HIGH FIBER

❧RECIPES❧

pil

Publications International, Ltd.

Pictured on the front cover: Wheat Berry Apple Salad *(page 70)*.
Pictured on the back cover *(left to right):* Ham & Egg Breakfast Panini *(page 16)* and English Bread Pudding *(page 120)*.

Contributing Writer: Marilyn Pocius

Photograph of adzuki beans on page 8 *(top right)* by Shutterstock.

ISBN-13: 978-1-4508-1867-4
ISBN-10: 1-4508-1867-6

Library of Congress Control Number: 2010940935

Manufactured in China.

8 7 6 5 4 3 2 1

Nutritional Analysis: Every effort has been made to check the accuracy of the nutritional information that appears with each recipe. However, because numerous variables account for a wide range of values for certain foods, nutritive analyses in this book should be considered approximate. Different results may be obtained by using different nutrient databases and different brand-name products.

Note: This book is for informational purposes and is not intended to provide medical advice. Neither Publications International, Ltd., nor the authors, editors or publisher takes responsibility for any possible consequences from any treatment, procedure, exercise, dietary modification, action, or applications of medication or preparation by any person reading or following the information in this cookbook. The publication of this book does not constitute the practice of medicine, and this cookbook does not replace your physician, pharmacist or health-care specialist. **Before undertaking any course of treatment or nutritional plan, the authors, editors and publisher advise the reader to check with a physician or other health-care provider.**

Publications International, Ltd.

Table of Contents

Is Fiber a Miracle Food?

The claims for fiber seem too good to be true. Can eating more fiber really help you lose weight, lower your cholesterol, prevent digestive problems and control your blood sugar? It may not be a miraculous solution to all these problems, but fiber can certainly help.

How Fiber Works

Simply put, fiber is the part of plant food our bodies can't use. That's why for decades fiber was pretty much ignored. It didn't provide nutrients and nobody was clamoring for more fiber in their food. In fact, food manufacturers went to great lengths to remove fiber from grains to make white bread and other processed foods softer and easier to digest. How the tide has turned! We now realize that fiber is vital for our health in many different ways. Food manufacturers are finding ways to add fiber to everything from bread to yogurt and boasting about it on their labels.

There are two kinds of fiber. *Soluble fiber* slows down the digestive process. It combines with water to form a kind of gel that binds with fatty acids and other substances in the digestive tract to prevent or lessen their absorption. This can help regulate blood sugar and lower cholesterol. *Insoluble fiber* bulks up to make you feel full and then moves through your digestive system to clear out toxins and keep you regular. Don't fret about the different kinds of fiber, though. We need both types and they are often both present in the same foods.

Five Easy Ways to Increase the Fiber in Your Diet:

1. Start out strong. Choose a high-fiber cereal with fruit for breakfast.

2. Switch to whole grains. Try whole grain breads and pastas.

3. Eat the whole fruit. Fiber is in the peel and the pulp.

4. Drop that peeler! Instead, scrub carrots and potatoes.

5. Eat beans or lentils three times a week. They're fiber heros.

How Much is Enough?

Most Americans eat about 11 grams of fiber a day. Current recommendations are for between 21 and 38 grams a day. The amount varies with age, gender and number of calories consumed. Needless to say, you're probably not getting enough! Add fiber to your diet gradually, though, or you may experience bloating or intestinal gas. It takes time for the natural bacteria in your digestive system to adjust to the change in diet. It also helps to drink plenty of water every day since fiber works best when it absorbs water.

Fiber and Weight Loss

Since our bodies can't absorb fiber, its calories don't count! Better yet, high-fiber foods make you feel fuller sooner and that feeling lasts longer. First, fiber takes a longer time to leave your stomach and you feel more satisfied with fewer calories. Then, as they travel through your digestive system, high-

fiber foods appear to trigger the release of a hormone known as CCK (cholecystokinin) that suppresses hunger. (It's the same hormone that's released and makes you feel satisfied after you eat a high-fat, high-protein food like steak.) Finally, fiber actually reduces the absorption of some of the other calories you consume with it. It binds to them so they are excreted along with the fiber.

But it Tastes Like Cardboard!

If you think the only way to eat more fiber is to bulk up on bran flakes, you are in for a delicious surprise. Luscious fruits like avocados, raspberries and bananas are high in fiber. You might not have too much trouble enjoying corn on the cob or a bowl of chili either—they're also high-fiber foods. Whole foods

are the best choices. A medium orange has 3 to 4 grams of fiber; orange juice has 0 grams. A baked potato eaten with the skin has 5 grams of fiber. Skip the skin and you'll only get about 2 grams. Generally, the more a food is processed, the lower its fiber content. Brown rice beats white; a fresh apple is better than applesauce.

Introduction

High-Fiber Fruits and Vegetables (1-cup serving)

 acorn squash - 6 g

 grapefruit,* one half - 2 g

 apple, large with skin - 5 g

 green peas - 9 g

 asparagus - 4 g

 orange* - 4 g

avocado, cubed - 10 g

pear, large with skin - 6 g

banana, medium - 3 g

potato, medium baked with skin - 5 g

broccoli - 2 g

 raspberries - 8 g

carrot - 4 g

 spinach, cooked - 4 g

corn - 5 g

strawberries - 4 g

most of the fiber in citrus is in the white pith

Surprise!

Coffee and chocolate both contain fiber.
Admittedly not a lot, but it's nice to know that a
cup of instant coffee or one ounce of chocolate
provides almost 2 grams of dietary fiber!

Whole Grain Goodness

All grains have three parts. There is a tough outer layer that protects the grain called the bran. The starchy endosperm makes up the biggest portion of the kernel. The germ of the grain is at its base. The bran and the germ contain the most fiber and nutrients; they are the parts often removed when grain is processed. Whole grains still contain all three parts.

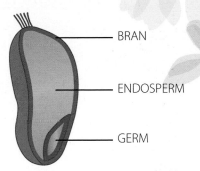

BRAN

ENDOSPERM

GERM

The easiest and most obvious way to add fiber to your life is to switch from white to whole wheat bread. Do read labels carefully, however, since "wheat flour" does NOT mean whole wheat flour. Multigrain breads are not necessarily whole grain either. It's wise to check the fiber count on the nutritional label.

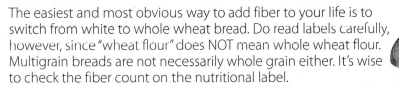

Beyond Wheat

Of course, whole grains aren't limited to breads. Switching to brown rice instead of white doubles the fiber. There are a number of pastas manufactured with whole wheat as well as lentils, flaxseed and other nutritious grains that add fiber. The taste differences from ordinary pasta are so subtle you might not even notice.

Quinoa is an amazing grain that was sacred to the ancient Incas and is now readily available. It's high in fiber and protein, has a sweet subtle taste and cooks in only 15 minutes. No wonder it's often called the "super grain."

Adding barley to your diet is another smart move. Slightly sweet, nutty and chewy, barley is easy to love and makes a good substitute for rice. Pearl (pearled) barley, which is the most available kind, has been

polished to remove its tough outer hull. Hulled or Scotch barley has more of the bran intact so is more nutritious but also takes longer to cook. In addition to being high in fiber, barley is also a good source of niacin and selenium.

Mediterranean Barley
Salad, pg 118

The Magical Bean

All kinds and colors of beans and lentils pack 10 grams of fiber or more in a one-cup serving. Add beans to salads, soups and tacos. Make bean dips. Try them refried, baked or mixed with rice. Beans are so versatile it's easy to add them to almost any meal. (After all, baked beans are part of a classic British breakfast.) As if that weren't enough, beans are also an excellent source of vitamins, minerals, proteins and antioxidants.

adzuki beans

These small, dark red beans are slightly sweet and creamy when cooked. They are the basis for sweet red bean paste used in Asian desserts.

black beans (turtle beans, frijoles negros)

Black beans are a staple of Latin American dishes. Their strong, earthy flavor and firm texture help them stand out in soups, salads and all sorts of side dishes.

chickpeas (garbanzo beans)

The versatile chickpea has an almost buttery flavor and is a nutritional powerhouse with over 80 nutrients, plus plenty of fiber and protein. Many classic vegetarian dishes, including hummus and falafel, are based on chickpeas.

kidney beans

Kidney beans are full-flavored and retain their kidney shape even with long cooking times. They are usually the bean of choice for chili or cold salads. They come in dark red, light red, pink or white (also called cannellini beans).

lentils

Lentils cook quickly and are often served puréed. The most common varieties are brown and red, but for a larger selection explore the many different kinds used in Indian or Middle Eastern cuisines.

white beans (Great Northern, navy beans)

These mild, meaty beans are favorites in casseroles, stews and soups.

Bean Counting

One pound of dried beans will yield four to five cups of cooked beans, or approximately 8 servings. A 15-ounce can contains between 1½ to 2 cups of cooked beans, depending on the variety.

Dried versus Canned

Both canned beans and dried beans cooked from scratch offer the same great fiber and nutrition. The exception is that canned beans can be high in sodium. You can reduce this sodium content substantially by thoroughly rinsing and draining the beans before you use them. Cooking dried beans takes more time, but it's easy, economical and produces firmer, tastier beans. Here are the steps.

1. Buy the right beans. Old beans or those that have been stored in heat or humidity will never cook correctly. (Throw away that old package that's been in your cupboard for five years right now!)

2. Sort through the beans and discard any broken ones or foreign matter while rinsing them. Cover with fresh cold water by about 3 inches. Toss any beans that float. Soak for at least 4 hours or until the bean skins get wrinkled. (If soaking longer than 10 hours, refrigerate the beans.)

3. Drain the beans, place them in a saucepan and cover with at least an inch of water. Bring to a boil and skim any foam that rises. Cover and simmer over low heat for 45 minutes to 2 hours or until tender but not mushy.

Beans, Beans the Musical Fruit

Let's be blunt: Beans have a reputation for creating intestinal gas. The reason for this phenomenon is that beans contain huge sugar molecules called oligosaccharides. These molecules pass through the small intestine undigested. In the large intestine, bacteria go to work and, as they do, gas is produced. To minimize the problem, add beans and all high-fiber foods to your diet gradually so your body has time to adjust.

Using this Book

Almost every recipe in this book provides 5 grams of fiber or more per serving. (A few baked goods have 4 grams.) Once you discover all the tasty ways to prepare high-fiber foods, you can easily add more of them to your everyday menus. Enjoy plenty of whole grains, fresh fruits and vegetables and you're well on the way. With the help of the recipes in this book you'll soon agree that high-fiber eating is not only easy and healthy, it's a delicious change for the better!

Sunny Seed Bran Waffles

      2 egg whites
      1 tablespoon dark brown sugar
      1 tablespoon vegetable oil
      1 cup fat-free (skim) milk
    ⅔ cup wheat bran
    ⅔ cup quick oats
  1½ teaspoons baking powder
    ¼ teaspoon salt
      3 tablespoons toasted sunflower seeds*
      1 cup apple butter

*To toast sunflower seeds, cook and stir sunflower seeds in small nonstick skillet over medium heat about 5 minutes or until golden brown.

1. Beat egg whites in medium bowl with electric mixer until soft peaks form. Blend brown sugar and oil in small bowl. Stir in milk; mix well.

2. Combine bran, oats, baking powder and salt in large bowl; mix well. Stir milk mixture into bran mixture. Add sunflower seeds; stir just until combined. *Do not overmix.* Gently fold in beaten egg whites.

3. Spray nonstick waffle iron lightly with nonstick cooking spray; heat according to manufacturer's directions. Stir batter; spoon ½ cup batter into waffle iron for each waffle. Cook until steam stops escaping from around edges and waffle is golden brown. Serve each waffle with ¼ cup apple butter.

Makes 4 waffles

NUTRIENTS PER SERVING: Fiber: 6g, Calories: 384, Fat: 10g, Carbohydrate: 68g, Protein: 12g

Mexican Breakfast Burrito

1 container (16 ounces) cholesterol-free egg substitute
⅛ teaspoon black pepper
   Nonstick cooking spray
⅓ cup drained black beans
2 tablespoons sliced green onion
2 (10-inch) flour tortillas
3 tablespoons shredded reduced-fat Cheddar cheese
3 tablespoons salsa

1. Whisk egg substitute and pepper in large bowl. Coat nonstick skillet with cooking spray; heat over medium heat. Pour egg mixture into skillet. Cook and stir 5 to 7 minutes or until egg mixture begins to set. Fold in beans and green onion. Cook and stir 3 minutes or until cooked through but still moist.

2. Spoon mixture down centers of tortillas; top with cheese. Fold in opposite sides of each tortilla; roll up burrito-style and cut in half. Top with salsa.

Makes 4 servings

NUTRIENTS PER SERVING: Fiber: 5g, Calories: 200, Fat: 1g, Carbohydrate: 22g, Protein: 17g

Breakfast Pom Smoothie

1 small ripe banana
½ cup mixed berries
¾ cup pomegranate juice
⅓ to ½ cup soymilk or milk

Blend banana and berries in blender or food processor until smooth. Add juice and soymilk; blend until smooth.

Makes 1 serving

Variations: Substitute pomegranate-blueberry juice for the pomegranate juice. Add 2 tablespoons plain yogurt, or substitute yogurt for the soymilk. Use all strawberries, blueberries, raspberries or blackberries instead of the mixed berries.

NUTRIENTS PER SERVING: Fiber: 6g, Calories: 253, Fat: 1g, Carbohydrate: 59g, Protein: 3g

Mexican Breakfast Burrito

Berry Bran Muffins

2 cups dry bran cereal
1¼ cups fat-free (skim) milk
½ cup packed brown sugar
¼ cup vegetable oil
1 egg, lightly beaten
1 teaspoon vanilla
1¼ cups all-purpose flour
1 tablespoon baking powder
¼ teaspoon salt
1 cup fresh or frozen blueberries (partially thawed if frozen)

1. Preheat oven to 350°F. Line 12 standard (2¾-inch) muffin cups with paper baking cups.

2. Mix cereal and milk in medium bowl. Let stand 5 minutes to soften. Add brown sugar, oil, egg and vanilla; beat well. Combine flour, baking powder and salt in large bowl. Stir in cereal mixture just until dry ingredients are moistened. Gently fold in blueberries. Fill prepared muffin cups almost full.

3. Bake 20 to 25 minutes (25 to 30 minutes if using frozen berries) or until toothpick inserted into centers comes out clean. Serve warm.

Makes 12 servings

Tip: Bran is the outer layer of a grain of wheat. It protects the wheat kernel and contains important fiber and nutrients. These are removed when the grain is processed to make white flour and the bran is removed. In general, the darker the grain, the more fiber. Choose products made with whole grains to get the most fiber and best nutrition.

NUTRIENTS PER SERVING: Fiber: 4g, Calories: 172, Fat: 5g, Carbohydrate: 29g, Protein: 4g

Berry Bran Muffins

Ham & Egg Breakfast Panini

    Nonstick cooking spray
¼ cup chopped green or red bell pepper
2 tablespoons sliced green onion
1 slice (1 ounce) reduced-fat smoked deli ham, chopped (¼ cup)
½ cup cholesterol-free egg substitute
    Black pepper
4 slices multigrain or whole grain bread
2 (¾-ounce) slices reduced-fat Cheddar cheese or Swiss cheese

1. Spray small skillet with cooking spray; heat over medium heat. Add bell pepper and green onion; cook and stir 4 minutes or until vegetables begin to soften. Stir in ham.

2. Combine egg substitute and black pepper in small bowl; pour into skillet. Cook and stir about 2 minutes or until egg mixture is almost set.

3. Spray one side of each bread slice with cooking spray; turn bread over. Top each of 2 bread slices with 1 cheese slice and half of egg mixture. Top with remaining bread slices.

4. Heat grill pan or medium skillet over medium heat. Grill sandwiches, pressing lightly with spatula, about 2 minutes per side or until toasted and cheese is melted. Cut sandwiches in half; serve immediately.

Makes 2 sandwiches

NUTRIENTS PER SERVING: Fiber: 6g, Calories: 271, Fat: 5g, Carbohydrate: 30g, Protein: 24g

Ham & Egg Breakfast Panini

French Toast with Sweet Butter and Orange-Spiked Fruit Topping

FRENCH TOAST
- 1½ cups cholesterol-free egg substitute
- 2 teaspoons canola oil, divided
- 8 slices Italian multigrain or whole wheat bread

SWEET BUTTER SPREAD
- ¼ cup reduced-fat margarine spread
- 2 teaspoons sugar substitute*
- 2 teaspoons grated orange peel
- 1 teaspoon ground cinnamon
- 1 teaspoon vanilla

FRUIT TOPPING
- 1½ cups strawberries, hulled and quartered
- 1 cup sliced bananas
- ¼ cup orange juice
- 1 tablespoon sugar substitute*

This recipe was tested using sucralose-based sugar substitute.

1. Preheat oven to 200°F. Pour egg substitute into shallow pie plate.

2. Heat 1 teaspoon oil in large nonstick skillet. Dip 4 bread slices into egg substitute; turn to coat. Add bread to skillet; cook about 2 minutes per side or until golden brown. Transfer to serving plate; place in oven to keep warm. Repeat with remaining oil and bread.

3. For Sweet Butter Spread, combine margarine, sugar substitute, orange peel, cinnamon and vanilla in small bowl; stir until well blended.

4. For Fruit Topping, combine strawberries, bananas, orange juice and sugar substitute in medium bowl; toss gently to coat. To serve, top each piece of French toast with about 1½ teaspoons Sweet Butter Spread and ¼ cup Fruit Topping.   *Makes 4 servings*

NUTRIENTS PER SERVING: Fiber: 10g, Calories: 337, Fat: 10g, Carbohydrate: 48g, Protein: 18g

French Toast with Sweet Butter and Orange-Spiked Fruit Topping

Breakfast Burgers

¾ pound extra-lean ground turkey
½ cup minced red bell pepper
½ cup minced green bell pepper
 2 teaspoons dried minced onion
 1 teaspoon dried parsley flakes
½ teaspoon black pepper
    Nonstick cooking spray
 2 tablespoons water
 4 whole wheat English muffins
 4 large spinach leaves
 4 slices soy cheese

1. Mix turkey, bell peppers, minced onion, parsley flakes and black pepper in large bowl. Shape mixture into 4 patties; spray with cooking spray.

2. Cook patties in large nonstick skillet over medium heat 7 minutes or until lightly browned on bottom. Turn and cook 7 minutes. Add water; cover and cook 3 minutes or until cooked through (165°F).

3. Toast English muffins. Place 1 spinach leaf, 1 turkey burger and 1 cheese slice on each muffin half; top with remaining muffin half.

Makes 4 servings

NUTRIENTS PER SERVING: Fiber: 5g, Calories: 300, Fat: 6g, Carbohydrate: 30g, Protein: 31g

Breakfast Burger

Date-Nut Granola

2 cups old-fashioned oats
2 cups barley flakes
1 cup sliced almonds
⅓ cup vegetable oil
⅓ cup honey
1 teaspoon vanilla
1 cup chopped dates

1. Preheat oven to 350°F. Grease 13×9-inch baking pan.

2. Combine oats, barley flakes and almonds in large bowl.

3. Combine oil, honey and vanilla in small bowl. Pour over oat mixture; stir well. Pour into prepared pan.

4. Bake about 25 minutes or until toasted, stirring frequently after the first 10 minutes. Stir in dates while mixture is still hot. Cool; store tightly covered.

Makes 12 servings

NUTRIENTS PER SERVING: Fiber: 7g, Calories: 330, Fat: 14g, Carbohydrate: 47g, Protein: 8g

Date-Nut Granola

Mexican Omelet Roll-Ups with Avocado Sauce

2 cups cholesterol-free egg substitute
2 tablespoons reduced-fat (2%) milk
1 tablespoon margarine
1½ cups (6 ounces) shredded Monterey Jack cheese
1 large tomato, seeded and chopped
¼ cup chopped fresh cilantro
8 corn tortillas
1½ cups salsa (optional)
2 medium avocados, chopped
¼ cup reduced-fat sour cream
2 tablespoons finely chopped onion
1 jalapeño or serrano pepper,* chopped (optional)
1 to 2 teaspoons lime juice
¼ teaspoon salt
¼ teaspoon minced garlic

Jalapeño peppers can sting and irritate the skin, so wear rubber gloves when handling peppers and do not touch your eyes.

1. Preheat oven to 350°F. Spray 13×9-inch baking dish with nonstick cooking spray.

2. Whisk egg substitute and milk in medium bowl until blended. Melt margarine in large skillet over medium heat. Add egg mixture to skillet. Cook and stir 5 minutes or until egg mixture is set, but still soft. Remove from heat. Stir in cheese, tomato and cilantro.

3. Spoon about ⅓ cup egg mixture evenly down center of each tortilla. Roll up tortillas and place, seam side down, in prepared dish. Pour salsa evenly over tortillas, if desired.

4. Cover tightly with foil and bake 20 minutes or until heated through.

5. Meanwhile, process avocados, sour cream, onion, jalapeño pepper, if desired, lime juice, salt and garlic in food processor or blender until smooth. Serve roll-ups with avocado sauce.   *Makes 8 servings*

Tip: To reduce amount of fat in recipe, omit avocado sauce and serve with additional salsa and fat-free sour cream.

NUTRIENTS PER SERVING: Fiber: 5g, Calories: 320, Fat: 21g, Carbohydrate: 19g, Protein: 15g

Mexican Omelet Roll-Ups with Avocado Sauce

Super Oatmeal

   2 cups water
2¾ cups old-fashioned oats
   ½ cup finely diced dried figs
   ⅓ cup lightly packed dark brown sugar
   ⅓ cup sliced almonds, toasted*
   ¼ cup flax seeds
   ½ teaspoon salt
   ½ teaspoon ground cinnamon
   2 cups reduced-fat (2%) or whole milk, plus additional for serving

To toast almonds, spread in single layer on baking sheet. Bake in preheated 350°F oven 8 to 10 minutes or until golden brown, stirring frequently.

1. Bring water to a boil in large saucepan over high heat. Stir in oats, figs, brown sugar, almonds, flax seeds, salt and cinnamon. Immediately add milk; stir well.

2. Reduce heat to medium-high. Cook and stir 5 to 7 minutes or until oatmeal is thick and creamy. Spoon into individual bowls. Serve with additional milk, if desired.   *Makes 5 to 6 servings*

Tip: Oatmeal is not only a delicious high-fiber food, it is high in soluble fiber which can help lower bad (LDL) cholesterol. Oatmeal is a simple whole food that contains a variety of vitamins, minerals and antioxidants and is good for you in almost any form except for certain sugary, flavored varieties. It's also quick and convenient. What a super way to start your day!

NUTRIENTS PER SERVING: Fiber: 9g, Calories: 380, Fat: 11g, Carbohydrate: 62g, Protein: 12g

---

Super Oatmeal

Breakfast Pepperoni Flats

  2 high-fiber low-fat flatbreads
  1 cup (4 ounces) shredded mozzarella cheese
  2 plum tomatoes, diced
 24 slices turkey pepperoni, cut into quarters
  2 teaspoons grated Parmesan cheese
  ¼ to ½ cup chopped fresh basil

1. Preheat oven to 425°F. Place flatbreads on large baking sheet. Sprinkle evenly with mozzarella, tomatoes, turkey pepperoni and Parmesan.

2. Bake 3 minutes or until cheese is melted. Sprinkle with basil. Let stand on baking sheet 2 minutes before cutting in half.   *Makes 4 servings*

NUTRIENTS PER SERVING: Fiber: 5g, Calories: 130, Fat: 4g, Carbohydrate: 9g, Protein: 15g

Veggie-Beef Hash

  4 ounces cooked roast beef, trimmed, finely chopped
 1½ cups frozen seasoning blend*
  1 cup shredded potatoes
  ½ cup shredded carrots
  1 egg white
  ½ teaspoon dried rosemary
  ½ teaspoon black pepper
    Nonstick cooking spray
  ½ cup salsa (optional)

Frozen seasoning blend is a combination of finely chopped onion, celery, green and red bell peppers and parsley flakes. Frozen or fresh sliced bell peppers and onion can be substituted.

1. Combine beef, seasoning blend, potatoes, carrots, egg white, rosemary and black pepper in large bowl.

2. Lightly spray large nonstick skillet with cooking spray; heat over medium-high heat. Add beef mixture; press down firmly to form large cake. Cook 4 minutes or until browned on bottom, pressing down on cake several times. Turn; cook 4 minutes or until lightly browned and heated through. Serve with salsa, if desired.   *Makes 2 servings*

NUTRIENTS PER SERVING: Fiber: 5g, Calories: 297, Fat: 9g, Carbohydrate: 33g, Protein: 22g

Breakfast Pepperoni Flat

Soups & Stews

Zesty Vegetarian Chili

1 tablespoon vegetable oil
1 large red bell pepper, coarsely chopped
2 medium zucchini or yellow squash (or 1 of each), cut into ½-inch
   chunks
4 cloves garlic, minced
1 can (about 14 ounces) fire-roasted diced tomatoes
¾ cup chunky salsa
2 teaspoons chili powder
1 teaspoon dried oregano
1 can (about 15 ounces) red kidney beans, rinsed and drained
10 ounces extra-firm tofu, well drained and cut into ½-inch cubes
   Chopped fresh cilantro (optional)

1. Heat oil in large saucepan over medium heat. Add bell pepper; cook and stir 4 minutes. Add zucchini and garlic; cook and stir 3 minutes.

2. Stir in tomatoes, salsa, chili powder and oregano; bring to a boil over high heat. Reduce heat; simmer 15 minutes or until vegetables are tender.

3. Stir beans into chili. Simmer 2 minutes or until heated through. Stir in tofu; remove from heat. Ladle into bowls; garnish with cilantro.

Makes 4 servings

Note: Tofu is made from the curds of soybean milk. It has a bland, slightly nutty taste, but readily takes on the flavor of foods it's cooked with. Cover any leftover tofu with water and refrigerate.

NUTRIENTS PER SERVING: **Fiber:** 8g, **Calories:** 231, **Fat:** 8g, **Carbohydrate:** 28g, **Protein:** 15g

Pumpkin Soup with Crumbled Bacon and Toasted Pumpkin Seeds

2 teaspoons olive oil
½ cup raw hulled pumpkin seeds
1 medium onion, chopped
1 teaspoon salt
½ teaspoon chipotle chili powder, or more to taste
½ teaspoon black pepper
2 cans (29 ounces each) solid-pack pumpkin
4 cups chicken broth
¾ cup apple cider
½ cup whipping cream
   Sour cream (optional)
3 slices thick-sliced bacon, crisp-cooked and crumbled

SLOW COOKER DIRECTIONS

1. Heat oil in medium skillet over medium heat. Add pumpkin seeds; cook and stir 1 minute or until seeds begin to pop. Transfer to small bowl; set aside.

2. Add onion to same skillet; cook and stir over medium heat until translucent. Stir in salt, chili powder and black pepper. Transfer to slow cooker. Whisk in pumpkin, broth and apple cider until smooth. Cover; cook on HIGH 4 hours.

3. Turn off slow cooker. Whisk in whipping cream; adjust seasonings. Strain, if desired. Garnish with sour cream, toasted pumpkin seeds and crumbled bacon.   *Makes 4 to 6 servings*

Tip: Hulled pumpkin seeds (or "pepitas") are a common ingredient in Mexican cooking. They can be purchased raw or roasted and salted.

NUTRIENTS PER SERVING: **Fiber:** 13g, **Calories:** 220, **Fat:** 10g, **Carbohydrate:** 29g, **Protein:** 10g

Pumpkin Soup with Crumbled Bacon and Toasted Pumpkin Seeds

Minestrone alla Milanese

1 cup diced potato
1 cup coarsely chopped carrots
2 cans (about 14 ounces each) reduced-sodium beef broth
1 can (about 14 ounces) diced tomatoes
1 cup coarsely chopped green cabbage
1 cup sliced zucchini
¾ cup chopped onion
¾ cup sliced fresh green beans
¾ cup coarsely chopped celery
¾ cup water
2 tablespoons olive oil
1 clove garlic, minced
½ teaspoon dried basil
¼ teaspoon dried rosemary
1 bay leaf
1 can (about 15 ounces) cannellini beans, rinsed and drained
Shredded Parmesan cheese (optional)

SLOW COOKER DIRECTIONS

1. Combine all ingredients except cannellini beans and cheese in slow cooker; mix well. Cover; cook on LOW 5 to 6 hours.

2. Add cannellini beans. Cover; cook on LOW 1 hour or until vegetables are tender.

3. Remove and discard bay leaf. Serve with cheese, if desired.

Makes 8 to 10 servings

NUTRIENTS PER SERVING: **Fiber:** 5g, **Calories:** 135, **Fat:** 4g, **Carbohydrate:** 23g, **Protein:** 8g

Minestrone alla Milanese

ve-Way Cincinnati Chili

 ...oked spaghetti, broken in half
 ...ound 80% lean ground beef
 2 cans (10 ounces each) diced tomatoes and green chiles
 1 can (about 15 ounces) red kidney beans, rinsed and drained
 1 can (10½ ounces) condensed French onion soup, undiluted
 1¼ cups water
 1 tablespoon chili powder
 1 teaspoon sugar
 ½ teaspoon salt
 ¼ teaspoon ground cinnamon
 ½ cup chopped onion
 ½ cup (2 ounces) shredded Cheddar cheese

1. Cook spaghetti according to package directions; drain.

2. Meanwhile, brown beef 6 to 8 minutes in large saucepan or Dutch oven over medium-high heat, stirring to break up meat; drain fat. Add tomatoes, beans, soup, water, chili powder, sugar, salt and cinnamon to saucepan; bring to a boil. Reduce heat to low. Simmer 10 minutes, stirring occasionally.

3. Serve chili over spaghetti; sprinkle with onion and cheese.

Makes 6 servings

Variation: Serve this traditional chili your way or one of the ways Cincinnatians do—two-way over spaghetti, three-way with cheese, four-way with cheese and chopped onion or five-way with beans added to the chili.

NUTRIENTS PER SERVING: **Fiber:** 5g, **Calories:** 609, **Fat:** 13g, **Carbohydrate:** 90g, **Protein:** 35g

---

Five-Way Cincinnati Chili

Italian Skillet Roasted Vegetable Soup

2 tablespoons olive oil, divided
1 medium red, yellow or orange bell pepper, chopped
1 clove garlic, minced
2 cups water
1 can (about 14 ounces) diced tomatoes
1 medium zucchini, thinly sliced
⅛ teaspoon red pepper flakes
1 can (about 15 ounces) navy beans, rinsed and drained
3 to 4 tablespoons chopped fresh basil
1 tablespoon balsamic vinegar
½ teaspoon liquid smoke (optional)
¾ teaspoon salt

1. Heat 1 tablespoon oil in Dutch oven over medium-high heat. Add bell pepper; cook and stir 4 minutes or until edges are browned. Add garlic; cook and stir 15 seconds. Add water, tomatoes, zucchini and pepper flakes. Bring to a boil over high heat. Reduce heat; cover and simmer 20 minutes.

2. Stir in beans, basil, remaining 1 tablespoon oil, vinegar, liquid smoke, if desired, and salt. Remove from heat. Let stand, covered, 10 minutes before serving.   *Makes 5 servings*

Tip: Navy beans are also called pea beans or Yankee beans. The name Navy comes from the fact that they've been served in the Navy since 1800. These are the small white beans used to make canned pork and beans. You could certainly substitute Great Northern or cannellini beans if you wished.

NUTRIENTS PER SERVING: **Fiber:** 6g, **Calories:** 157, **Fat:** 3g, **Carbohydrate:** 25g, **Protein:** 8g

Italian Skillet Roasted Vegetable Soup

Bean Ragoût with Cilantro-Cornmeal Dumplings

     2 cans (about 14 ounces each) diced tomatoes
     1 can (about 15 ounces) pinto or kidney beans, rinsed and drained
     1 can (about 15 ounces) black beans, rinsed and drained
  1½ cups chopped red bell peppers
     1 large onion, chopped
     2 small zucchini, sliced
     ½ cup chopped green bell pepper
     ½ cup chopped celery
     1 poblano pepper, seeded and chopped
     2 cloves garlic, minced
     3 tablespoons chili powder
     2 teaspoons ground cumin
     1 teaspoon dried oregano
     ¼ teaspoon salt
     ⅛ teaspoon black pepper
        Cilantro-Cornmeal Dumplings (recipe follows)

SLOW COOKER DIRECTIONS

1. Combine tomatoes, beans, red bell peppers, onion, zucchini, green bell pepper, celery, poblano pepper, garlic, chili powder, cumin, oregano, salt and black pepper in slow cooker; mix well. Cover; cook on LOW 7 to 8 hours.

2. Prepare dumplings 1 hour before serving. *Turn slow cooker to HIGH.* Drop dumplings by level tablespoonfuls (larger dumplings will not cook properly) on top of ragoût. Cover; cook 1 hour or until toothpick inserted into dumplings comes out clean. *Makes 6 servings*

Cilantro-Cornmeal Dumplings

     ¼ cup all-purpose flour
     ¼ cup yellow cornmeal
     ½ teaspoon baking powder
     ¼ teaspoon salt
     1 tablespoon shortening
     1 tablespoon shredded Cheddar cheese
     2 teaspoons minced fresh cilantro
     ¼ cup milk

Mix flour, cornmeal, baking powder and salt in medium bowl. Cut in shortening with pastry blender or two knives until mixture resembles coarse crumbs. Stir in cheese and cilantro. Stir in milk just until dry ingredients are moistened.

NUTRIENTS PER SERVING: **Fiber:** 10g, **Calories:** 294, **Fat:** 6g, **Carbohydrate:** 54g, **Protein:** 17g

---

Mushroom Barley Stew

1 tablespoon olive oil
1 medium onion, finely chopped
1 cup chopped carrots (about 2 carrots)
1 clove garlic, minced
5 cups reduced-sodium vegetable broth
1 cup uncooked pearl barley
1 cup dried wild mushrooms, broken into pieces
1 teaspoon salt
½ teaspoon dried thyme
½ teaspoon black pepper

SLOW COOKER DIRECTIONS

1. Heat oil in medium skillet over medium-high heat. Add onion, carrots and garlic; cook and stir 5 minutes or until tender. Transfer to slow cooker.

2. Add broth, barley, mushrooms, salt, thyme and pepper to slow cooker; stir well to combine. Cover; cook on LOW 6 to 7 hours. Adjust seasonings.

Makes 4 to 6 servings

Variation: To turn this thick robust stew into a soup, add 2 to 3 additional cups of broth. Cook the same length of time.

NUTRIENTS PER SERVING: **Fiber:** 12g, **Calories:** 310, **Fat:** 5g, **Carbohydrate:** 59g, **Protein:** 10g

---

Chicken Soup au Pistou

Olive oil cooking spray
½ pound boneless skinless chicken breasts, cut into ½-inch pieces
1 large onion, diced
3 cans (about 14 ounces each) chicken broth
1 can (about 15 ounces) Great Northern beans, rinsed and drained
1 can (about 14 ounces) whole tomatoes, undrained
2 medium carrots, sliced
1 large potato, diced
¼ teaspoon salt
¼ teaspoon black pepper
1 cup fresh or frozen green beans, cut into 1-inch pieces
¼ cup prepared pesto
Grated Parmesan cheese (optional)

1. Spray large saucepan with cooking spray; heat over medium-high heat. Add chicken; cook and stir about 5 minutes or until chicken is browned. Add onion; cook and stir 2 minutes.

2. Add broth, Great Northern beans, tomatoes with juice, carrots, potato, salt and pepper. Bring to a boil, stirring to break up tomatoes. Reduce heat to low. Cover and simmer 15 minutes, stirring occasionally. Add green beans; cook 5 minutes or until vegetables are tender.

3. Top each serving with 1½ teaspoons pesto and sprinkle with Parmesan cheese, if desired. *Makes 8 servings*

NUTRIENTS PER SERVING: **Fiber:** 5g, **Calories:** 164, **Fat:** 6g, **Carbohydrate:** 18g, **Protein:** 12g

Chicken Soup au Pistou

Jamaican Black Bean Stew

2 cups uncooked brown rice
2 pounds sweet potatoes
3 pounds butternut squash
1 large onion, coarsely chopped
1 can (about 14 ounces) vegetable broth
3 cloves garlic, minced
1 tablespoon curry powder
1½ teaspoons ground allspice
½ teaspoon ground red pepper
¼ teaspoon salt
2 cans (about 15 ounces each) black beans, rinsed and drained
½ cup raisins
3 tablespoons lime juice
1 cup diced tomato
1 cup diced peeled cucumber

1. Prepare rice according to package directions. Meanwhile, peel sweet potatoes; cut into ¾-inch chunks to measure 4 cups. Peel squash; remove seeds. Cut into ¾-inch cubes to measure 5 cups.

2. Combine sweet potatoes, squash, onion, broth, garlic, curry powder, allspice, pepper and salt in Dutch oven. Bring to a boil; reduce heat to low. Cover and simmer 15 minutes or until sweet potatoes and squash are tender. Add beans and raisins; simmer 5 minutes or until heated through. Stir in lime juice.

3. Serve stew over rice; top with tomato and cucumber.   *Makes 8 servings*

NUTRIENTS PER SERVING: **Fiber:** 10g, **Calories:** 463, **Fat:** 4g, **Carbohydrate:** 102g, **Protein:** 16g

---

Jamaican Black Bean Stew

Lentil Chili

1 tablespoon canola oil
4 cloves garlic, minced
1 tablespoon chili powder
1 package (32 ounces) reduced-sodium vegetable broth
¾ cup dried green or brown lentils, rinsed and sorted
2 teaspoons hot pepper sauce
2 cups peeled and diced butternut squash
1 can (about 14 ounces) diced tomatoes
½ cup chopped fresh cilantro
¼ cup hulled pumpkin seeds (optional)

1. Heat oil in large saucepan over medium heat. Add garlic; cook and stir 1 minute. Stir in chili powder; cook and stir 30 seconds.

2. Add broth, lentils and hot pepper sauce; bring to a boil over high heat. Reduce heat and simmer 15 minutes. Stir in squash and tomatoes; simmer 18 to 20 minutes or until lentils and squash are tender.

3. Ladle into bowls; top with cilantro and pumpkin seeds, if desired.

Makes 5 servings

Note: Lentils are not only a good source of iron and protein, but are packed with dietary fiber. The soluble fiber in lentils helps to stabilize blood sugar levels while the insoluble fiber is known to lower high cholesterol levels and promote digestive health. Pumpkin seeds add a nice crunch to the meal for an additional 36 calories, 3 grams of fat, 2 grams of protein, and less than 1 gram of carbohydrate (for 2½ teaspoons). They're a good source of plant sterols, which have been found to promote heart health.

NUTRIENTS PER SERVING: **Fiber:** 12g, **Calories:** 184, **Fat:** 3g, **Carbohydrate:** 32g, **Protein:** 10g

---

Lentil Chili

Curried Eggplant, Squash & Chickpea Stew

1 teaspoon olive oil
½ cup diced red bell pepper
¼ cup diced onion
1¼ teaspoons curry powder
1 clove garlic, minced
½ teaspoon salt
1¼ cups cubed peeled eggplant
¾ cup cubed peeled acorn or butternut squash
⅔ cup rinsed and drained canned chickpeas
½ cup vegetable broth or water
3 tablespoons white wine
Hot pepper sauce (optional)
¼ cup lemon sugar-free yogurt
2 tablespoons chopped fresh parsley

1. Heat oil in medium saucepan over medium heat. Add bell pepper and onion; cook and stir 5 minutes. Stir in curry powder, garlic and salt; cook and stir 1 minute. Add eggplant, squash, chickpeas, broth and wine. Cover; bring to a boil. Reduce heat and simmer 20 to 25 minutes or until eggplant and squash are tender.

2. Season to taste with pepper sauce, if desired. Serve with yogurt and parsley. *Makes 2 servings*

Tip: The versatile chickpea (also known as garbanzo bean) has an almost buttery flavor and is a nutritional powerhouse with over 80 nutrients, plus fiber and protein. Many classic vegetarian dishes, including hummus and falafel, are made from chickpeas.

NUTRIENTS PER SERVING: **Fiber:** 10g, **Calories:** 216, **Fat:** 4g, **Carbohydrate:** 38g, **Protein:** 7g

Curried Eggplant, Squash & Chickpea Stew

Greens, White Bean and Barley Soup

   2 tablespoons olive oil
   3 carrots, diced
1½ cups chopped onions
   2 cloves garlic, minced
1½ cups sliced mushrooms
   6 cups vegetable broth
   2 cups cooked barley
   1 can (about 15 ounces) Great Northern beans, rinsed and drained
   2 bay leaves
   1 teaspoon sugar
   1 teaspoon dried thyme
   7 cups chopped stemmed collard greens (about 24 ounces)
   1 tablespoon white wine vinegar
     Hot pepper sauce
     Red bell pepper strips (optional)

1. Heat oil in Dutch oven over medium heat. Add carrots, onions and garlic; cook and stir 3 minutes. Add mushrooms; cook and stir 5 minutes or until carrots are tender.

2. Add broth, barley, beans, bay leaves, sugar and thyme. Bring to a boil over high heat. Reduce heat to medium-low; cover and simmer 5 minutes. Add greens; simmer 10 minutes. Remove and discard bay leaves. Stir in vinegar. Season with hot pepper sauce. Garnish with bell pepper strips.

Makes 8 servings

NUTRIENTS PER SERVING: **Fiber:** 8g, **Calories:** 226, **Fat:** 4g, **Carbohydrate:** 36g, **Protein:** 9g

Greens, White Bean and Barley Soup

Taco Stew

Nonstick cooking spray
½ pound 95% lean ground beef
1 cup chopped onion
1 can (16 ounces) pinto beans in Mexican-style sauce
1 can (about 14 ounces) stewed tomatoes, undrained
1 can (10 ounces) diced tomatoes with green chiles
2 teaspoons chili powder
5 (8-inch) corn tortillas
5 cups shredded iceberg lettuce
½ cup (2 ounces) shredded reduced-fat sharp Cheddar cheese
¼ cup chopped fresh cilantro (optional)

1. Preheat oven to 350°F. Spray large saucepan with cooking spray; heat over medium-high heat. Add beef and onion. Brown beef 6 to 8 minutes, stirring to break up meat; drain fat. Add beans, stewed tomatoes with juice, diced tomatoes and chili powder. Bring to a boil. Reduce heat to low. Cover and simmer 10 minutes.

2. Meanwhile, cut each tortilla into 6 wedges; place on baking sheet. Spray tortilla wedges lightly on both sides with cooking spray. Bake 5 minutes.

3. Divide lettuce among soup bowls. Ladle beef mixture evenly over lettuce. Top with cheese and cilantro, if desired. Serve with tortilla wedges.

Makes 5 servings

NUTRIENTS PER SERVING: **Fiber:** 9g, **Calories:** 328, **Fat:** 11g, **Carbohydrate:** 38g, **Protein:** 20g

---

Taco Stew

Whole Grain Goodness

Quinoa with Roasted Vegetables

Nonstick cooking spray
2 medium sweet potatoes, cut into ½-inch-thick slices
1 medium eggplant, cut into ½-inch cubes
1 medium tomato, cut into wedges
1 large green bell pepper, sliced
1 small onion, cut into wedges
½ teaspoon salt
¼ teaspoon black pepper
¼ teaspoon ground red pepper
1 cup uncooked quinoa
2 cloves garlic, minced
½ teaspoon dried thyme
¼ teaspoon dried marjoram
2 cups water or reduced-sodium vegetable broth

1. Preheat oven to 450°F. Line large jelly-roll pan with foil; spray with cooking spray.

2. Arrange sweet potatoes, eggplant, tomato, bell pepper and onion on prepared pan; spray lightly with cooking spray. Sprinkle with salt, black pepper and ground red pepper; toss to coat. Bake 20 to 30 minutes or until vegetables are browned and tender.

3. Meanwhile, place quinoa in fine-mesh strainer; rinse well under cold running water. Spray medium saucepan with cooking spray; heat over medium heat. Add garlic, thyme and marjoram; cook and stir 1 to 2 minutes. Add quinoa; cook and stir 2 to 3 minutes. Stir in water; bring to a boil over high heat. Reduce heat to low. Simmer, covered, 15 to 20 minutes or until water is absorbed. Transfer quinoa to large bowl; gently stir in vegetables.

Makes 6 servings

NUTRIENTS PER SERVING: Fiber: 6g, Calories: 193, Fat: 2g, Carbohydrate: 40g, Protein: 6g

Hoppin' Shrimp and Brown Rice

1 bag boil-in-bag instant brown rice
  Nonstick cooking spray
2 cups frozen black-eyed peas
2 cups reduced-sodium vegetable broth
2 cups salsa
1 can (about 14 ounces) diced tomatoes
1 bag (12 ounces) cooked baby shrimp
1 box (10 ounces) frozen whole okra
4 stalks celery, trimmed and chopped
¼ cup chopped red onion
¼ cup chopped fresh cilantro
  Juice of ½ lime
½ teaspoon black pepper
  Lime wedges (optional)

1. Prepare rice according to package directions.

2. Spray large skillet with cooking spray. Add black-eyed peas, broth, salsa, tomatoes, shrimp, okra, celery, onion, cilantro, lime juice and black pepper. Simmer over medium-high heat 20 minutes or until heated through, stirring occasionally.

3. Serve shrimp mixture topped with rice. Garnish with lime wedges.

Makes 4 servings

Apricot Coleslaw: If desired, serve with Apricot Coleslaw. Whisk ¼ cup balsamic vinegar, 2 tablespoons extra-virgin olive oil, ¼ cup sugar-free apricot preserves, ¼ cup chopped fresh basil, ½ teaspoon minced garlic and ¼ teaspoon black pepper in large bowl. Toss with 3 cups coleslaw mix.

NUTRIENTS PER SERVING: Fiber: 9g, Calories: 386, Fat: 3g, Carbohydrate: 61g, Protein: 30g

---

Hoppin' Shrimp and Brown Rice

Whole Wheat Penne Pasta with Summer Vegetables

    6 ounces uncooked whole wheat penne pasta (about 2 cups)
    2 teaspoons olive oil
    2 cloves garlic, minced
 1½ cups fresh broccoli florets
    1 medium zucchini, chopped (about 1¼ cups)
    ½ medium yellow bell pepper, chopped (about ¾ cup)
 1½ cups cherry or grape tomatoes, halved
    1 cup mushrooms, sliced
    ½ teaspoon dried oregano
    ¾ cup crumbled reduced-fat feta cheese

1. Cook pasta according to package directions, omitting fat. Drain and keep warm.

2. Heat oil in large nonstick skillet over medium-high heat. Add garlic, broccoli, zucchini and bell pepper. Cook and stir 2 minutes or until vegetables begin to soften.

3. Add tomatoes, mushrooms and oregano; mix well. Reduce heat to medium; cook and stir about 8 minutes or until vegetables are tender and tomatoes release their juices.

4. Combine vegetables with pasta. Toss in feta cheese.   *Makes 4 servings*

NUTRIENTS PER SERVING: **Fiber:** 7g, **Calories:** 264, **Fat:** 7g, **Carbohydrate:** 41g, **Protein:** 15g

Whole Wheat Penne Pasta with Summer Vegetables

Vegetarian Paella

aspoons canola oil
1 cup chopped onion
2 cloves garlic, minced
1 cup uncooked brown rice
2¼ cups vegetable broth
1 teaspoon Italian seasoning
¾ teaspoon salt
½ teaspoon ground turmeric
⅛ teaspoon ground red pepper
1 can (about 14 ounces) stewed tomatoes, undrained
1 cup chopped red bell pepper
1 cup coarsely chopped carrots
1 can (14 ounces) quartered artichoke hearts, drained
1 small zucchini, halved and sliced
½ cup frozen baby peas

1. Heat oil in large nonstick skillet over medium-high heat. Add onion and garlic; cook and stir 6 to 7 minutes or until tender. Reduce heat to medium and stir in rice. Cook 1 minute, stirring constantly.

2. Add broth, Italian seasoning, salt, turmeric and ground red pepper. Bring to a boil. Reduce heat to medium-low. Simmer, covered, 30 minutes. Stir in tomatoes with their juices, bell pepper and carrots; simmer, covered, 10 minutes. Reduce heat to low and stir in artichoke hearts, zucchini and peas. Cook, covered, 10 minutes or until vegetables are crisp-tender.

Makes 6 servings

NUTRIENTS PER SERVING: Fiber: 7g, Calories: 241, Fat: 7g, Carbohydrate: 43g, Protein: 5g

Vegetarian Paella

Italian Eggplant with Millet and Pepper Stuffing

¼ cup uncooked millet
2 small eggplants (about ¾ pound total)
¼ cup chopped red bell pepper, divided
¼ cup chopped green bell pepper, divided
1 teaspoon olive oil
1 clove garlic, minced
1½ cups reduced-sodium vegetable broth
½ teaspoon ground cumin
½ teaspoon dried oregano
⅛ teaspoon red pepper flakes

1. Cook and stir millet in large heavy skillet over medium heat 5 minutes or until golden. Transfer to small bowl; set aside.

2. Cut eggplants lengthwise into halves. Scoop out flesh, leaving about ¼-inch-thick shell. Reserve shells; chop eggplant flesh. Combine 1 teaspoon red bell pepper and 1 teaspoon green bell pepper in small bowl; set aside.

3. Heat oil in same skillet over medium heat. Add chopped eggplant, remaining red and green bell pepper and garlic; cook and stir about 8 minutes or until eggplant is tender.

4. Stir in toasted millet, broth, cumin, oregano and red pepper flakes. Bring to a boil over high heat. Reduce heat to medium-low. Cook, covered, 35 minutes or until all liquid has been absorbed and millet is tender. Remove from heat; let stand, covered, 10 minutes.

5. Preheat oven to 350°F. Pour 1 cup water into 8-inch square baking pan. Fill eggplant shells with eggplant-millet mixture. Sprinkle with reserved chopped bell peppers, pressing in lightly. Carefully place filled shells in prepared pan. Bake 15 minutes or until heated through.   *Makes 4 servings*

NUTRIENTS PER SERVING: Fiber: 7g, Calories: 122, Fat: 3g, Carbohydrate: 20g, Protein: 6g

Honey Whole Grain Bread

3 cups whole wheat flour, divided
2 cups warm (not hot) whole milk
¾ to 1 cup all-purpose flour, divided
¼ cup honey
2 tablespoons vegetable oil
1 package (¼ ounce) active dry yeast
¾ teaspoon salt

SLOW COOKER DIRECTIONS

1. Spray 1-quart casserole, soufflé dish or other high-sided baking pan that fits into slow cooker with nonstick cooking spray. Combine 1½ cups whole wheat flour, milk, ½ cup all-purpose flour, honey, oil, yeast and salt in large bowl. Beat with electric mixer at medium speed 2 minutes.

2. Add remaining 1½ cups whole wheat flour and ¼ cup to ½ cup all-purpose flour until dough is no longer sticky. (If mixer has difficulty mixing dough, mix in remaining flours with wooden spoon.) Transfer to prepared dish.

3. Make foil handles with strips of heavy-duty foil. Criss-cross 3 or 4 strips and place in slow cooker. Place dish on strips. Cover; cook on HIGH 3 hours or until edges are browned.

4. Use foil handles to lift dish from slow cooker. Let stand 5 minutes. Unmold on wire rack to cool.   *Makes 8 to 10 servings*

NUTRIENTS PER SERVING: Fiber: 6g, Calories: 297, Fat: 6g, Carbohydrate: 53g, Protein: 10g

Barley, Bean and Corn Frittata

2 cups water
½ cup uncooked pearl barley
¾ teaspoon salt, divided
2 teaspoons olive oil
1 can (about 15 ounces) black beans, rinsed and drained
2 cups (8 ounces) shredded Cheddar cheese, divided
¾ cup corn
½ cup chopped green bell pepper
¼ cup chopped fresh cilantro
7 eggs *or* 1¾ cups cholesterol-free egg substitute
1 cup cottage cheese
½ teaspoon ground red pepper
1 cup salsa
   Sour cream (optional)

1. Bring water to a boil in medium saucepan over high heat. Add barley and ¼ teaspoon salt. Reduce heat to low. Cover and simmer 40 to 45 minutes or until tender. Remove from heat. Let stand, covered, 5 minutes. Drain.

2. Preheat oven to 400°F. Brush large cast iron or ovenproof skillet with oil. Layer barley, beans, 1 cup Cheddar cheese, corn, bell pepper and cilantro in skillet. Blend eggs, cottage cheese, remaining ½ teaspoon salt and ground red pepper in blender or food processor just until smooth. Carefully pour egg mixture into skillet.

3. Bake 30 minutes or until egg mixture is set. Sprinkle with remaining 1 cup Cheddar cheese. Bake 5 minutes or until cheese is melted. Spoon salsa evenly over top. Let stand 5 minutes before cutting into wedges. Garnish with sour cream. *Makes 6 to 8 servings*

NUTRIENTS PER SERVING: Fiber: 7g, Calories: 404, Fat: 21g, Carbohydrate: 31g, Protein: 27g

Barley, Bean and Corn Frittata

Spicy Chickpeas & Couscous

1 can (about 14 ounces) vegetable broth
1 teaspoon ground coriander
½ teaspoon ground cardamom
½ teaspoon ground turmeric
½ teaspoon hot pepper sauce
¼ teaspoon salt
⅛ teaspoon ground cinnamon
1 cup matchstick-size carrots
1 can (about 15 ounces) chickpeas, rinsed and drained
1 cup frozen green peas
1 cup uncooked couscous
2 tablespoons chopped fresh mint or parsley

1. Combine broth, coriander, cardamom, turmeric, pepper sauce, salt and cinnamon in large saucepan; bring to a boil over high heat. Add carrots; reduce heat and simmer 5 minutes.

2. Add chickpeas and green peas; simmer 2 minutes.

3. Stir in couscous. Cover; remove from heat. Let stand 5 minutes or until liquid is absorbed. Sprinkle with mint.   *Makes 6 servings*

Tip: Although couscous is often referred to as a grain, it is actually made of semolina flour rolled into tiny granules. This makes couscous similar to pasta. For an even higher fiber count, use whole wheat couscous instead of regular. All couscous is presteamed and ready to eat in a matter of minutes.

NUTRIENTS PER SERVING: Fiber: 10g, **Calories:** 226, **Fat:** 2g, Carbohydrate: 44g, **Protein:** 9g

Spicy Chickpeas & Couscous

Bulgur Pilaf with Tomato and Zucchini

1 cup bulgur wheat
1 tablespoon olive oil
¾ cup chopped onion
2 cloves garlic, minced
1 can (about 14 ounces) whole tomatoes, drained and coarsely
    chopped
½ pound zucchini (2 small), thinly sliced
1 cup reduced-sodium vegetable or chicken broth
1 teaspoon dried basil
⅛ teaspoon black pepper

1. Rinse bulgur thoroughly under cold water, removing any debris. Drain well; set aside.

2. Heat oil in large saucepan over medium heat. Add onion and garlic; cook and stir 3 minutes or until onion is tender. Stir in tomatoes and zucchini; reduce heat to medium-low. Cook, covered, 10 to 15 minutes or until zucchini is almost tender, stirring occasionally.

3. Stir bulgur, broth, basil and pepper into vegetable mixture. Bring to a boil over high heat. Cover; remove from heat. Let stand 10 minutes or until liquid is absorbed. Stir gently before serving. *Makes 8 servings*

NUTRIENTS PER SERVING: Fiber: 5g, Calories: 98, Fat: 2g, Carbohydrate: 18g, Protein: 3g

Bulgur Pilaf with Tomato and Zucchini

Wheat Berry Apple Salad

1 cup uncooked wheat berries (whole wheat kernels)
½ teaspoon salt
2 apples (1 red and 1 green)
½ cup dried cranberries
⅓ cup chopped walnuts
1 stalk celery, chopped
   Grated peel and juice of 1 medium orange
2 tablespoons rice wine vinegar
1½ tablespoons chopped fresh mint
   Lettuce leaves (optional)

1. Place wheat berries and salt in large saucepan; cover with 1 inch water.* Bring to a boil. Stir and reduce heat to low. Cover and cook, stirring occasionally, 45 minutes to 1 hour or until wheat berries are tender but chewy. (Add additional water if wheat berries become dry during cooking.) Drain and let cool. (Refrigerate for up to 4 days if not using immediately.)

2. Cut unpeeled apples into bite-size pieces. Combine wheat berries, apples, cranberries, walnuts, celery, orange peel, orange juice, vinegar and mint in large bowl. Cover; refrigerate at least 1 hour to allow flavors to blend. Serve on lettuce leaves, if desired. *Makes 6 servings*

To cut cooking time by 20 to 30 minutes, wheat berries may be soaked in water overnight. Drain and cover with 1 inch fresh water before cooking.

NUTRIENTS PER SERVING: Fiber: 5g, Calories: 193, Fat: 6g, Carbohydrate: 33g, Protein: 6g

Wheat Berry Apple Salad

Mediterranean Pita Sandwiches

1 cup plain fat-free yogurt
1 tablespoon chopped fresh cilantro
2 cloves garlic, minced
1 teaspoon lemon juice
1 can (about 15 ounces) chickpeas, rinsed and drained
1 can (14 ounces) artichoke hearts, drained and coarsely chopped
1½ cups thinly sliced cucumber halves
½ cup shredded carrot
½ cup chopped green onions
4 rounds whole wheat pita bread, cut in half

1. Combine yogurt, cilantro, garlic and lemon juice in small bowl.

2. Combine chickpeas, artichoke hearts, cucumbers, carrot and green onions in medium bowl. Stir in yogurt mixture until well blended.

3. Divide cucumber mixture among pita halves.   *Makes 4 servings*

Tip: We don't usually think about adding artichokes to a salad or sandwich. That's a shame because they add a bit of sophisticated Mediterranean flavor and a good helping of fiber, too. The terms artichoke hearts and artichoke bottoms are used interchangeably. They both refer to the round fleshy base of the artichoke.

NUTRIENTS PER SERVING: **Fiber:** 16g, **Calories:** 399, **Fat:** 3g, **Carbohydrate:** 79g, **Protein:** 19g

Mediterranean Pita Sandwiches

Healthy Main Courses

Soba Stir-Fry

8 ounces uncooked soba (buckwheat) noodles
1 tablespoon olive oil
2 cups sliced shiitake mushrooms
1 medium red bell pepper, cut into thin strips
2 whole dried red chiles *or* ¼ teaspoon red pepper flakes
1 clove garlic, minced
2 cups shredded napa cabbage
½ cup reduced-sodium vegetable or chicken broth
2 tablespoons tamari or soy sauce
1 tablespoon rice wine or dry sherry
2 teaspoons cornstarch
1 package (14 ounces) firm tofu, drained and cut into 1-inch cubes
2 green onions, thinly sliced

1. Cook noodles according to package directions. Drain and set aside.

2. Heat oil in large nonstick skillet or wok over medium heat. Add mushrooms, bell pepper, dried chiles and garlic. Cook and stir 3 minutes or until mushrooms are tender. Add cabbage. Cover; cook 2 minutes or until cabbage is wilted.

3. Combine broth, tamari, rice wine and cornstarch in small bowl. Stir sauce into vegetable mixture. Cook 2 minutes or until sauce is thickened.

4. Stir in tofu and noodles; toss gently until heated through. Remove whole chiles. Sprinkle with green onions. Serve immediately.   *Makes 4 servings*

NUTRIENTS PER SERVING: Fiber: 6g, Calories: 443, Fat: 13g, Carbohydrate: 64g, Protein: 27g

Vegetable Risotto

2 tablespoons olive oil, divided
1 medium zucchini, cubed
1 medium yellow squash, cubed
1 cup sliced stemmed shiitake mushrooms
1 cup chopped onion
1 clove garlic, minced
3 plum tomatoes, seeded and chopped
1 teaspoon dried oregano
3 cups vegetable broth
1 cup uncooked arborio rice
¼ cup grated Parmesan cheese
  Salt and black pepper (optional)
½ cup frozen peas, thawed

1. Heat 1 tablespoon oil in large saucepan over medium heat. Add zucchini and yellow squash; cook and stir 5 minutes or until crisp-tender. Transfer to medium bowl; set aside.

2. Add mushrooms, onion and garlic to saucepan; cook and stir 5 minutes or until tender. Add tomatoes and oregano; cook and stir 2 to 3 minutes or until tomatoes are soft. Transfer to bowl with zucchini mixture.

3. Heat broth in small saucepan over medium-low heat; keep hot.

4. Meanwhile, heat remaining 1 tablespoon oil in large saucepan over medium heat. Add rice; cook and stir 2 minutes.

5. Using ladle or measuring cup, add about ¾ cup broth to rice. Cook and stir until broth is absorbed. Repeat with remaining broth. Cook until rice is tender, but not mushy. Total cooking time will be 20 to 25 minutes.

6. Stir cheese into rice mixture. Season to taste with salt and pepper, if desired. Stir in reserved vegetables and peas; cook until heated through. Serve immediately.   *Makes 4 to 6 servings*

NUTRIENTS PER SERVING: Fiber: 5g, Calories: 394, Fat: 9g, Carbohydrate: 56g, Protein: 10g

Vegetable Risotto

Seasoned Chicken with Beans and Rice

1 teaspoon vegetable oil
½ cup chopped green onions
1 teaspoon minced garlic
1½ cups reduced-sodium chicken broth
2 tablespoons all-purpose flour
3 cups frozen mixed vegetables
1 can (about 15 ounces) kidney beans, rinsed and drained
1 cup shredded cooked chicken
1 teaspoon dried rosemary
½ teaspoon dried thyme
⅛ teaspoon ground red pepper
2 cups hot cooked brown rice

1. Heat oil in large nonstick skillet over medium heat. Add green onions and garlic; cook 1 minute.

2. Whisk broth and flour together in medium bowl; add to skillet. Add frozen vegetables, beans, chicken, rosemary, thyme and red pepper; bring to a boil. Reduce heat and simmer, covered, 6 minutes or until vegetables are tender. Serve over brown rice.   *Makes 4 servings*

Tip: Red kidney beans are full flavored and retain their kidney shape even with long cooking times. They are often the bean of choice for chili or salad. White kidney beans are usually referred to by their more appealing Italian name—cannellini beans.

NUTRIENTS PER SERVING: Fiber: 14g, Calories: 397, Fat: 5g, Carbohydrate: 58g, Protein: 31g

Seasoned Chicken with Beans and Rice

Mu Shu Vegetables

3 tablespoons reduced-sodium soy sauce
2 tablespoons dry sherry
1½ tablespoons minced fresh ginger
2 teaspoons cornstarch
3 cloves garlic, minced
1½ teaspoons sesame oil
1 tablespoon peanut oil
3 leeks, cut into pieces
3 carrots, julienned
1 cup thinly sliced fresh shiitake mushrooms
1 small head napa or savoy cabbage, shredded (about 4 cups)
2 cups mung bean sprouts, rinsed and drained
8 ounces firm tofu, drained and cut into thin strips
12 (8-inch) fat-free flour tortillas, warmed*
Prepared peanut sauce
¾ cup finely chopped honey-roasted peanuts

Tortillas can be warmed in microwave just before using. Stack tortillas and wrap in plastic wrap. Microwave on HIGH 30 seconds to 1 minute, turning over and rotating a quarter turn once during heating.

1. Combine soy sauce, sherry, ginger, cornstarch, garlic and sesame oil in small bowl until smooth; set aside.

2. Heat peanut oil in wok over medium-high heat. Add leeks, carrots and mushrooms; stir-fry 2 minutes. Add cabbage; stir-fry 3 minutes or until tender. Add bean sprouts and tofu; stir-fry 1 minute or until hot. Stir soy sauce mixture; add to wok. Cook and stir 1 minute or until sauce is thickened.

3. Spread each tortilla with about 1 teaspoon peanut sauce. Spoon ½ cup vegetable mixture onto bottom half of each tortilla; sprinkle with 1 tablespoon peanuts.

4. Fold bottom of tortilla over filling; fold in sides and roll up. Serve with additional peanut sauce.   *Makes 6 servings*

NUTRIENTS PER SERVING: Fiber: 18g, Calories: 477, Fat: 18g, Carbohydrate: 64g, Protein: 19g

Mu Shu Vegetables

South American Chicken and Quinoa

Tomato-Apricot Chutney (recipe follows)
1 teaspoon ground turmeric
1 teaspoon dried thyme
¾ teaspoon salt, divided
1 pound boneless skinless chicken breasts, cut into 1-inch pieces
2 tablespoons olive oil, divided
1 large red or green bell pepper, chopped
1 medium onion, chopped
1 cup uncooked quinoa
1 cup chicken broth
1 cup unsweetened coconut milk
1 teaspoon curry powder
¼ teaspoon ground ginger

1. Prepare Tomato-Apricot Chutney; set aside.

2. Combine turmeric, thyme and ¼ teaspoon salt in shallow dish. Dip one chicken piece at a time into spice mixture, coating all sides; set aside.

3. Heat 1 tablespoon oil in large skillet over medium-high heat. Add bell pepper and onion. Cook and stir 2 minutes or until vegetables are crisp-tender. Remove to bowl with slotted spoon.

4. Add remaining 1 tablespoon oil to skillet. Add chicken pieces. Cook and stir 5 minutes or until browned and cooked through. Set aside.

5. Place quinoa in fine-mesh strainer; rinse well under cold running water. Combine quinoa, broth, coconut milk, curry powder, remaining ½ teaspoon salt and ginger in large saucepan. Bring to a boil over high heat. Reduce heat to low; simmer, covered, 10 minutes.

6. Stir in chicken and bell pepper mixture; cook 5 minutes or until liquid is absorbed. Serve with Tomato-Apricot Chutney.   *Makes 4 servings*

Tomato-Apricot Chutney: Combine ¾ cup apple cider, ¾ cup finely diced dried apricots, ½ cup currants and 3 tablespoons cider vinegar in medium saucepan. Bring to a boil. Reduce heat to low; simmer, covered, 10 minutes. Drain 1 can (about 14 ounces) diced tomatoes. Stir tomatoes, 1 tablespoon brown sugar, 1 teaspoon ground ginger and ⅛ teaspoon ground cloves into saucepan. Simmer 5 minutes or until liquid is absorbed.

NUTRIENTS PER SERVING: Fiber: 9g, Calories: 676, Fat: 25g, Carbohydrate: 77g, Protein: 36g

South American Chicken and Quinoa

Couscous-Stuffed Squash

2 small acorn squash, halved lengthwise and seeded
1 medium poblano pepper, sliced
1 small onion, sliced
1¼ cups vegetable broth
½ cup shiitake mushrooms, chopped
¾ cup uncooked couscous
1 medium plum tomato, diced
2 tablespoons pine nuts

1. Preheat oven to 400°F. Spray baking sheet with nonstick cooking spray; place squash, cut side down, on baking sheet. Arrange pepper and onion on baking sheet. Cover with foil; bake 35 to 40 minutes or until squash is tender.

2. Bring broth and mushrooms to a boil in medium saucepan over medium-high heat. Stir in couscous, tomato and pine nuts; cover and remove from heat. Let stand 5 minutes. Meanwhile, dice roasted pepper and onion; add to couscous mixture. Fluff couscous with fork.

3. Turn squash cut side up. Fill each half with about ¾ cup couscous mixture.

Makes 4 servings

Tip: Acorn squash have thick, hard skins that can be difficult to cut. To make cutting easier, soften them in the microwave. Pierce the skin with a fork; microwave on HIGH 1 to 2 minutes. Allow to cool for a few minutes, then slice lengthwise and remove the seeds.

NUTRIENTS PER SERVING: Fiber: 6g, Calories: 290, Fat: 4g, Carbohydrate: 57g, Protein: 9g

Couscous-Stuffed Squash

Vegetable Fajitas with Spicy Salsa

SALSA

3 medium tomatoes
1 small onion, unpeeled
1 jalapeño pepper
6 cloves garlic, unpeeled
Juice of 1 lime
1 teaspoon salt

FAJITAS

12 (8-inch) flour tortillas
1 tablespoon vegetable oil
4 medium bell peppers, cut into strips
1 medium red onion, thickly sliced
1 teaspoon salt
Black pepper
1 can (16 ounces) refried beans

1. Preheat broiler. Line baking sheet with parchment paper or foil. Place tomatoes, unpeeled onion, jalapeño and garlic on prepared baking sheet. Broil 10 minutes. Turn vegetables and rotate pan. Broil 10 minutes or until blackened. Cool 10 minutes. Peel vegetables and seed jalapeño. Place in blender or food processor with lime juice and salt; process to desired consistency. Refrigerate salsa until ready to serve.

2. Heat large heavy skillet over medium-high heat. Heat tortillas, one at a time, for 15 seconds or until browned; keep warm.

3. Add oil to skillet; reduce heat to medium. Add bell pepper strips and red onion slices; season with salt and black pepper. Cook and stir 10 minutes or until onion is cooked through and bell peppers are crisp-tender.

4. Heat refried beans in small saucepan. Spread about 2 tablespoons beans on each tortilla. Top with ⅓ cup vegetables and about 2 tablespoons salsa. Roll up; serve immediately.

Makes 6 servings

NUTRIENTS PER SERVING: Fiber: 6g, Calories: 292, Fat: 7g, Carbohydrate: 49g, Protein: 9g

Vegetable Fajitas with Spicy Salsa

Hot Three-Bean Casserole

2 tablespoons olive oil
1 cup coarsely chopped onion
1 cup chopped celery
2 cloves garlic, minced
1 can (about 15 ounces) chickpeas, rinsed and drained
1 can (about 15 ounces) kidney beans, rinsed and drained
1 cup coarsely chopped tomato
1 can (about 8 ounces) tomato sauce
1 cup water
1 to 2 jalapeño peppers,* minced
1 tablespoon chili powder
2 teaspoons sugar
1½ teaspoons ground cumin
1 teaspoon salt
1 teaspoon dried oregano
¼ teaspoon black pepper
2½ cups (10 ounces) frozen cut green beans
Fresh oregano (optional)

Jalapeño peppers can sting and irritate the skin, so wear rubber gloves when handling peppers and do not touch your eyes.

1. Heat oil in large skillet over medium heat. Add onion, celery and garlic; cook and stir 5 minutes or until tender.

2. Add chickpeas, kidney beans, tomato, tomato sauce, water, jalapeño pepper, chili powder, sugar, cumin, salt, dried oregano and black pepper. Bring to a boil. Reduce heat to low; simmer 20 minutes. Add green beans; simmer 10 minutes or until tender. Garnish with fresh oregano.

Makes 12 servings

NUTRIENTS PER SERVING: Fiber: 6g, Calories: 118, Fat: 3g, Carbohydrate: 20g, Protein: 6g

Hot Three-Bean Casserole

Chickpea Burgers

1 can (about 15 ounces) chickpeas, rinsed and drained
⅓ cup chopped carrot
⅓ cup herbed croutons
¼ cup chopped fresh parsley
¼ cup chopped onion
1 egg white
1 teaspoon minced garlic
1 teaspoon grated lemon peel
½ teaspoon black pepper
⅛ teaspoon salt
   Nonstick cooking spray
4 whole grain hamburger buns
   Tomato slices, lettuce leaves and salsa (optional)

1. Place chickpeas, carrot, croutons, parsley, onion, egg white, garlic, lemon peel, pepper and salt in food processor; process until blended. Shape mixture into 4 patties.

2. Spray large nonstick skillet with cooking spray; heat over medium heat. Cook patties 4 to 5 minutes or until bottoms are browned. Spray tops of patties with cooking spray; turn and cook 4 to 5 minutes or until browned.

3. Serve burgers on buns with tomato, lettuce and salsa, if desired.

Makes 4 servings

Tip: These Chickpea Burgers would be great served with just about any sort of prepared salsa, but for a special treat, make your own mango salsa. Simply combine chopped mango, onion and tomato with seasonings and some lime juice or vinegar. Refrigerate the salsa until ready to serve.

NUTRIENTS PER SERVING: Fiber: 7g, Calories: 271, Fat: 5g, Carbohydrate: 48g, Protein: 11g

Chickpea Burger

Veggie Tostadas

1 tablespoon olive oil
1 cup chopped onion
1 cup chopped celery
2 cloves garlic, chopped
1 can (about 15 ounces) red kidney beans, rinsed and drained
1 can (about 15 ounces) Great Northern beans, rinsed and drained
1 can (about 14 ounces) salsa-style diced tomatoes
2 teaspoons mild chili powder
1 teaspoon ground cumin
6 (6-inch) corn tortillas
   Toppings: chopped fresh cilantro, shredded lettuce, chopped
       seeded fresh tomatoes, shredded Cheddar cheese and sour
       cream (optional)

1. Heat oil in large skillet over medium heat. Add onion, celery and garlic.
Cook and stir 8 minutes or until softened. Stir in beans and tomatoes.
Add chili powder and cumin; stir. Reduce heat to medium-low. Simmer
30 minutes or until thickened, stirring occasionally.

2. Meanwhile, preheat oven to 400°F. Place tortillas in single layer directly
on oven rack. Bake 10 to 12 minutes or until crisp. Place one tortilla on
each plate. Spoon bean mixture evenly over each tortilla. Top with cilantro,
lettuce, tomatoes, Cheddar cheese and sour cream, if desired.

Makes 6 servings

NUTRIENTS PER SERVING: Fiber: 10g, Calories: 208, Fat: 3g,
Carbohydrate: 39g, Protein: 10g

Veggie Tostada

Black Bean & Rice Stuffed Poblano Peppers

2 large or 4 small poblano peppers
½ (15-ounce) can black beans, rinsed and drained
½ cup cooked brown rice
⅓ cup chunky salsa
⅓ cup shredded reduced-fat Cheddar cheese or pepper Jack cheese, divided

1. Preheat oven to 375°F. Spray shallow baking pan with nonstick cooking spray.

2. Cut thin slice from one side of each pepper. Chop pepper slices; set aside. Bring water to a boil in medium saucepan. Add whole peppers and boil 6 minutes. Drain and rinse with cold water. Remove and discard seeds and membranes.

3. Stir together beans, rice, salsa, chopped pepper and ¼ cup cheese in large bowl. Spoon into peppers; place in prepared pan. Cover with foil.

4. Bake 12 to 15 minutes or until heated through. Sprinkle with remaining cheese. Bake 2 minutes or until cheese melts. *Makes 2 servings*

Tip: Poblano chile peppers have dark green, almost black, skins that are as shiny as patent leather. They are fairly mild with a fresh, herbaceous flavor and are often used for stuffing. Look for firm, shiny peppers without wrinkles. In their dried form, poblanos are called ancho chiles.

NUTRIENTS PER SERVING: Fiber: 5g, Calories: 236, Fat: 4g, Carbohydrate: 38g, Protein: 14g

---

Black Bean & Rice Stuffed Poblano Peppers

Spicy African Chickpea and Sweet Potato Stew

        Spice Paste (recipe follows)
1½ pounds sweet potatoes, peeled and cubed
    2 cups vegetable broth or water
    1 can (about 15 ounces) chickpeas, rinsed and drained
    1 can (about 14 ounces) whole tomatoes, undrained, chopped
1½ cups sliced fresh okra *or* 1 package (10 ounces) frozen cut okra,
        thawed
        Cooked couscous
        Hot pepper sauce
        Fresh cilantro (optional)

1. Prepare Spice Paste.

2. Combine sweet potatoes, broth, chickpeas, tomatoes with juice, okra and Spice Paste in large saucepan. Bring to a boil over high heat. Reduce heat to low. Cover and simmer 15 minutes. Uncover; simmer 10 minutes or until vegetables are tender.

3. Serve stew with couscous and hot pepper sauce. Garnish with cilantro.

Makes 4 servings

Spice Paste

    6 cloves garlic, peeled
    1 teaspoon coarse salt
    2 tablespoons paprika
1½ teaspoons whole cumin seeds
    1 teaspoon black pepper
    ½ teaspoon ground ginger
    ½ teaspoon ground allspice
    1 tablespoon olive oil

Process garlic and salt in blender or small food processor until garlic is finely chopped. Add remaining seasonings; process 15 seconds. With blender running, pour in oil through cover opening; process until paste forms.

NUTRIENTS PER SERVING: Fiber: 14g, Calories: 546, Fat: 7g, Carbohydrate: 107g, Protein: 16g

Spicy African Chickpea and Sweet Potato Stew

Turkey Breast with Barley-Cranberry Stuffing

2 cups reduced-sodium chicken broth
1 cup quick-cooking barley
½ cup chopped onion
½ cup dried cranberries
2 tablespoons slivered almonds, toasted
½ teaspoon rubbed sage
½ teaspoon garlic-pepper seasoning
Nonstick cooking spray
1 fresh or thawed frozen bone-in turkey breast half
(about 2 pounds), skinned
⅓ cup finely chopped fresh parsley

SLOW COOKER DIRECTIONS

1. Combine broth, barley, onion, cranberries, almonds, sage and garlic-pepper seasoning in slow cooker.

2. Spray large nonstick skillet with cooking spray. Brown turkey breast over medium heat on all sides; add to slow cooker. Cover; cook on LOW 4 to 6 hours.

3. Transfer turkey to cutting board; cover with foil and let stand 10 to 15 minutes before carving. Stir parsley into mixture in slow cooker. Serve sliced turkey with stuffing and sauce.   *Makes 6 servings*

NUTRIENTS PER SERVING: Fiber: 6g, Calories: 298, Fat: 5g, Carbohydrate: 33g, Protein: 31g

Turkey Breast with Barley-Cranberry Stuffing

Sirloin Steak Antipasto Salad

  3 cloves garlic, minced
 ½ teaspoon black pepper
  1 beef top sirloin steak (about 1 pound), trimmed of fat
  8 cups torn romaine lettuce
16 cherry tomatoes, halved
16 pitted kalamata olives, halved lengthwise
  1 can (14 ounces) quartered artichoke hearts in water, drained
 ⅓ cup fat-free Italian or Caesar salad dressing
 ¼ cup fresh basil, cut into thin strips

1. Prepare grill for direct cooking or preheat broiler. Sprinkle garlic and pepper over steak.

2. Grill steak over medium-hot coals or broil 4 inches from heat 4 minutes per side for medium-rare or until desired doneness. Transfer steak to cutting board; tent with foil. Let stand 5 minutes.

3. Meanwhile, combine lettuce, tomatoes, olives and artichoke hearts in large bowl. Add dressing; toss well. Transfer to serving plates.

4. Cut steak crosswise into thin slices; arrange over salads. Drizzle juices from cutting board over steak. Sprinkle with basil.   *Makes 4 servings*

Tip: Beef top sirloin steak is a versatile cut of meat that can be grilled, broiled or cooked in a skillet. It is quite tender since it is cut from a portion of the cow that is near the tenderloin. Slicing it across the grain enhances this tenderness.

NUTRIENTS PER SERVING: **Fiber:** 9g, **Calories:** 250, **Fat:** 7g, **Carbohydrate:** 21g, **Protein:** 30g

Beans and Greens with Curry

1 cup adzuki beans*
4 cups plus 2 tablespoons cold water, plus additional for soaking
2 pounds Swiss chard or kale
1 tablespoon olive oil
½ cup diced white onion
2 cloves garlic, minced
2 teaspoons sweet or spicy curry powder
¼ teaspoon salt
¼ teaspoon black pepper

Adzuki beans are small reddish beans with a sweet flavor and high protein content. They are used in Japanese cooking and can be found at natural food markets.

1. Soak beans overnight in enough water to cover by at least 2 inches. Drain beans and rinse well.

2. Place beans in large saucepan with 4 cups water; bring to a boil. Reduce heat and simmer 40 to 60 minutes or until beans are tender. Drain beans; set aside.

3. Remove stems and ribs from greens and tear into large pieces.

4. Heat oil in large deep skillet over medium heat. Add onion and garlic; cook and stir 5 minutes or until onion is soft and translucent. Add curry powder; cook and stir 30 seconds or until slightly toasted and aromatic.

5. Add greens to skillet. Sprinkle with 2 tablespoons water. Cook 5 minutes or until wilted.

6. Add beans to chard mixture; cook and stir until heated through. Season with salt and pepper.

Makes 6 servings

NUTRIENTS PER SERVING: **Fiber:** 7g, **Calories:** 160, **Fat:** 3g, **Carbohydrate:** 27g, **Protein:** 9g

Beans and Greens with Curry

Quinoa and Roasted Corn

1 cup uncooked quinoa
2 cups water
½ teaspoon salt
4 ears corn *or* 2 cups frozen corn
¼ cup plus 1 tablespoon vegetable oil, divided
1 cup chopped green onions, divided
1 teaspoon coarse salt
1 cup quartered grape tomatoes or chopped plum tomatoes, drained*
1 cup black beans, rinsed and drained
¼ teaspoon grated lime peel
　Juice of 1 lime (about 2 tablespoons)
¼ teaspoon sugar
¼ teaspoon ground cumin
¼ teaspoon black pepper

Place tomatoes in fine-mesh strainer and place over bowl 10 to 15 minutes.

1. Place quinoa in fine-mesh strainer; rinse well under cold running water. Transfer to medium saucepan; add water and ½ teaspoon salt. Bring to a boil over high heat. Reduce heat; cover and simmer 15 to 18 minutes or until water is absorbed and quinoa is tender. Transfer quinoa to large bowl.

2. Meanwhile, remove husks and silk from corn; cut kernels off cobs. Heat ¼ cup oil in large skillet over medium-high heat. Add corn; cook 10 to 12 minutes or until tender and light brown, stirring occasionally. Stir in ⅔ cup green onions and coarse salt; cook and stir 2 minutes. Add corn to quinoa. Gently stir in tomatoes and black beans.

3. Combine lime peel, lime juice, sugar, cumin and pepper in small bowl. Whisk in remaining 1 tablespoon oil until blended. Pour over quinoa mixture; toss lightly to coat. Sprinkle with remaining ⅓ cup green onions. Serve warm or chilled.

Makes 6 to 8 servings

NUTRIENTS PER SERVING: **Fiber:** 6g, **Calories:** 285, **Fat:** 14g, **Carbohydrate:** 37g, **Protein:** 8g

Quinoa and Roasted Corn

Bulgur Salad Niçoise

2 cups water
¼ teaspoon salt
1 cup bulgur wheat
1 cup halved cherry tomatoes
1 can (6 ounces) tuna packed in water, drained and flaked
½ cup pitted black Niçoise olives*
3 tablespoons finely chopped green onions
1 tablespoon chopped fresh mint leaves (optional)
1½ tablespoons lemon juice
1 tablespoon olive oil
⅛ teaspoon black pepper
Mint leaves (optional)

If you use larger olives, slice or chop as desired.

1. Bring water and salt to a boil in medium saucepan. Stir in bulgur. Remove from heat. Cover and let stand 10 to 15 minutes or until water is absorbed and bulgur is tender. Fluff with fork.

2. Combine bulgur, tomatoes, tuna, olives, green onions and chopped mint, if desired, in large bowl. Combine lemon juice, oil and pepper in small bowl. Pour over salad. Toss gently to mix well. Garnish with mint leaves, if desired.

Makes 3 to 4 servings

Tip: To make bulgur wheat, whole wheat kernels are steamed, dried and ground to varying degrees. The fine grind, which is the most common type, is ready in a matter of minutes. Bulgur wheat is a whole grain and is a nutritious staple in Middle Eastern cooking. Tabbouleh is the best known recipe example.

NUTRIENTS PER SERVING: **Fiber:** 10g, **Calories:** 307, **Fat:** 8g, **Carbohydrate:** 40g, **Protein:** 21g

Bulgur Salad Niçoise

French Lentil Salad

1½ cups dried lentils, rinsed and sorted
¼ cup chopped walnuts
4 green onions, finely chopped
3 tablespoons balsamic vinegar
2 tablespoons chopped fresh parsley
1 tablespoon olive oil
¾ teaspoon salt
½ teaspoon dried thyme
¼ teaspoon black pepper
    Lettuce leaves (optional)

1. Place lentils in large saucepan; add water to cover by 2 inches. Bring to a boil over high heat. Cover; reduce heat and simmer 30 minutes or until lentils are tender, but not mushy, stirring occasionally. Drain lentils.

2. Meanwhile, preheat oven to 375°F. Spread walnuts in even layer on baking sheet. Bake 5 minutes or until lightly browned. Cool completely on baking sheet.

3. Combine lentils, green onions, vinegar, parsley, oil, salt, thyme and pepper in large bowl. Cover; refrigerate 1 hour or until cool.

4. Serve on lettuce leaves, if desired. Top with toasted walnuts before serving.   *Makes 4 servings*

Tip: Rinsing and sorting lentils is necessary since they can contain bits of dirt and even small stones, which can look a lot like lentils. Chances are you won't find any foreign objects in most lentils, since they are cleaned after harvesting. Still, it's worth a quick check for that one time in a dozen that there is something that needs to be removed.

NUTRIENTS PER SERVING: **Fiber:** 8g, **Calories:** 264, **Fat:** 8g, **Carbohydrate:** 34g, **Protein:** 16g

---

French Lentil Salad

Cheesy Baked Barley

2 cups water
½ cup uncooked pearl barley
½ teaspoon salt, divided
    Nonstick cooking spray
½ cup chopped onion
½ cup diced zucchini
½ cup diced red bell pepper
1½ teaspoons all-purpose flour
¾ cup fat-free (skim) milk
1 cup (4 ounces) shredded reduced-fat Italian cheese blend, divided
1 tablespoon Dijon mustard
    Black pepper

1. Bring water to a boil in small saucepan. Add barley and ¼ teaspoon salt. Cover; reduce heat and simmer 45 minutes or until barley is tender and water is absorbed. Remove from heat. Let stand, covered, 5 minutes.

2. Preheat oven to 375°F. Spray large skillet with cooking spray. Cook and stir onion, zucchini and bell pepper over medium-low heat about 10 minutes or until soft. Stir in flour and remaining ¼ teaspoon salt; cook 1 to 2 minutes. Add milk, stirring constantly; cook and stir until slightly thickened. Remove from heat. Add barley, ¾ cup cheese and mustard; stir until cheese is melted. Season with black pepper.

3. Spread in even layer in casserole. Sprinkle with remaining ¼ cup cheese. Bake 20 minutes or until hot. Preheat broiler. Broil casserole 1 to 2 minutes or until cheese is lightly browned. *Makes 2 servings*

NUTRIENTS PER SERVING: **Fiber:** 6g, **Calories:** 362, **Fat:** 9g, **Carbohydrate:** 50g, **Protein:** 20g

---

Moroccan Chickpeas

  1 cup chopped onion
  ¼ cup reduced-sodium vegetable broth
  2 cloves garlic, crushed
  2 cans (about 15 ounces each) chickpeas, rinsed and drained
  1 can (28 ounces) diced tomatoes
  ½ cup sliced red bell pepper
  ½ cup sliced yellow bell pepper
  ½ cup sliced green bell pepper
  2 tablespoons oil-cured olives, pitted and chopped
  1 teaspoon ground cumin
  1 teaspoon ground ginger
  1 teaspoon ground turmeric
  1 bay leaf
  2 tablespoons lemon juice
    Salt and black pepper

1. Combine onion, broth and garlic in large nonstick skillet. Cook and stir over medium heat 3 minutes or until onion softens.

2. Add chickpeas, tomatoes, bell peppers, olives, cumin, ginger, turmeric and bay leaf. Stir well. Simmer 5 minutes or until bell peppers are tender. Remove and discard bay leaf. Stir in lemon juice. Season with salt and black pepper.

Makes 6 servings

NUTRIENTS PER SERVING: Fiber: 8g, **Calories:** 219, **Fat:** 2g, Carbohydrate: 42g, **Protein:** 9g

---

Layered Taco Salad

nstick cooking spray
½ pound 95% lean ground beef
1½ teaspoons chili powder
1½ teaspoons ground cumin, divided
½ cup picante sauce
1 teaspoon sugar
6 cups shredded romaine lettuce
2 plum tomatoes, seeded and diced
½ cup chopped green onions
¼ cup chopped fresh cilantro
2 ounces (about 28) nacho-flavored baked tortilla chips, crumbled
½ cup fat-free sour cream
½ cup (2 ounces) shredded reduced-fat sharp Cheddar cheese or
    Mexican cheese blend

1. Spray medium nonstick skillet with cooking spray; heat over medium-high heat. Brown beef 6 to 8 minutes, stirring to break up meat; drain fat. Stir in chili powder and 1 teaspoon cumin. Let cool.

2. Combine picante sauce, sugar and remaining ½ teaspoon cumin in small bowl.

3. Place lettuce in 11×7-inch casserole. Layer with beef, tomatoes, green onions, cilantro and chips. Top with sour cream; sprinkle with cheese. Spoon picante sauce mixture on top.   *Makes 4 servings*

NUTRIENTS PER SERVING: **Fiber:** 5g, **Calories:** 258, **Fat:** 9g, **Carbohydrate:** 25g, **Protein:** 21g

---

Layered Taco Salad

Greek Pasta Salad

    6 cups cooked multigrain or whole wheat rotini or penne pasta
 1½ cups diced cucumber
    2 medium tomatoes, diced
    1 medium green bell pepper, diced
    2 ounces feta cheese, finely crumbled
  12 medium pitted black olives, sliced into thirds
  ¼ cup chopped fresh dill
     Juice of ½ lemon
  ¼ teaspoon salt
  ⅛ teaspoon black pepper

Mix all ingredients together in large bowl. Cover and refrigerate until ready
to serve.   *Makes 8 servings*

NUTRIENTS PER SERVING: **Fiber:** 5g, **Calories:** 202, **Fat:** 4g,
Carbohydrate: 35g, **Protein:** 7g

Wilted Spinach Salad with White Beans & Olives

    2 thick slices bacon, diced
  ½ cup chopped onion
    1 can (about 15 ounces) navy beans, rinsed and drained
  ½ cup halved pitted kalamata or black olives
    1 package (9 ounces) baby spinach
    1 cup cherry tomatoes (cut in half if large)
 1½ tablespoons balsamic vinegar
     Black pepper (optional)

1. Cook bacon in Dutch oven or large saucepan over medium heat
2 minutes. Add onion; cook, stirring occasionally, 5 to 6 minutes or until
bacon is crisp and onion is tender. Stir in beans and olives; heat through.

2. Add spinach, tomatoes and vinegar; cover and cook 1 minute or until
spinach is slightly wilted. Remove from heat; toss lightly. Transfer to serving
plates. Season with pepper, if desired.   *Makes 4 servings*

NUTRIENTS PER SERVING: **Fiber:** 14g, **Calories:** 230, **Fat:** 5g,
Carbohydrate: 35g, **Protein:** 13g

Greek Pasta Salad

Sweet Curried Chicken and Quinoa Salad

⅓ cup uncooked quinoa
1 cup water
2 tablespoons sliced almonds
   Nonstick cooking spray
4 ounces boneless skinless chicken breast, cut into bite-size pieces
1 tablespoon plus 1½ teaspoons light mayonnaise
1 tablespoon plus 1½ teaspoons fat-free sour cream
1½ teaspoons sugar substitute*
1 teaspoon curry powder
¼ teaspoon ground cumin
⅛ teaspoon salt
½ cup very thinly sliced celery
¼ cup finely chopped red onion
3 tablespoons golden raisins or regular raisins
   Baby spinach leaves

This recipe was tested using sucralose-based sugar substitute.

1. Place quinoa in fine mesh strainer; rinse well under cold running water. Combine quinoa and 1 cup water in small saucepan. Bring to a boil over high heat. Reduce heat to medium-low. Cover and simmer 15 to 18 minutes or until liquid is absorbed and quinoa is tender. Let cool.

2. Cook and stir almonds in large nonstick skillet over medium-high heat 3 to 4 minutes or until lightly browned. Set aside on plate. Coat skillet with cooking spray. Add chicken; cook and stir 3 to 5 minutes or until cooked through. Let cool.

3. Combine mayonnaise, sour cream, sugar substitute, curry powder, cumin and salt in medium bowl. Stir until well blended. Stir in celery, onion and raisins.

4. Add chicken, almonds and quinoa. Toss; let stand 10 minutes to blend flavors. Serve over spinach leaves.   *Makes 2 servings*

NUTRIENTS PER SERVING: **Fiber:** 5g, **Calories:** 326, **Fat:** 11g, **Carbohydrate:** 38g, **Protein:** 21g

---

Sweet Curried Chicken and Quinoa Salad

Mediterranean Barley Salad

1⅓ cups water
⅔ cup quick-cooking barley
½ cup diced roasted red peppers
12 pitted kalamata olives, coarsely chopped
12 turkey pepperoni slices, halved
¼ cup chopped red onion
2 ounces crumbled reduced-fat feta cheese
1 teaspoon dried basil
¼ teaspoon red pepper flakes
1 can (about 15 ounces) navy beans
1 can (14 ounces) sliced hearts of palm, drained
1 tablespoon extra virgin olive oil
1 tablespoon cider vinegar
Salt and black pepper

1. Bring water to a boil in medium saucepan over high heat. Add barley; reduce heat. Cover and simmer 15 minutes or until barley is tender.

2. Meanwhile, combine roasted peppers, olives, pepperoni, onion, feta, basil and red pepper flakes in medium bowl.

3. Place barley and beans in colander; run under cold water until barley is cool. Add barley, beans, hearts of palm, oil, vinegar, salt and pepper to roasted pepper mixture; toss gently. Cover and refrigerate until serving.

Makes 4 servings

NUTRIENTS PER SERVING: **Fiber:** 12g, **Calories:** 370, **Fat:** 9g, **Carbohydrate:** 57g, **Protein:** 20g

---

Mediterranean Barley Salad

Smart Sweets

English Bread Pudding

16 slices day-old, firm-textured white bread (1 small loaf)
1¾ cups milk
1 package (8 ounces) mixed dried fruit, cut into small pieces
½ cup chopped nuts
1 medium apple, chopped
⅓ cup packed brown sugar
¼ cup (½ stick) butter, melted
1 egg, lightly beaten
1 teaspoon ground cinnamon
¼ teaspoon ground nutmeg
¼ teaspoon ground cloves

SLOW COOKER DIRECTIONS

1. Tear bread, with crusts, into 1- to 2-inch pieces; place in slow cooker. Pour milk over bread; let soak 30 minutes. Stir in dried fruit, nuts and apple.

2. Combine brown sugar, butter, egg, cinnamon, nutmeg and cloves in small bowl; pour over bread mixture. Stir well to blend. Cover; cook on LOW 3½ to 4 hours or until skewer inserted into center of pudding comes out clean.

Makes 6 to 8 servings

Tip: Chopping dried fruit can be difficult. To make the job easier, cut the fruit with kitchen scissors. Spray the scissors or a chef's knife with nonstick cooking spray before chopping to prevent sticking.

NUTRIENTS PER SERVING: **Fiber:** 5g, **Calories:** 516, **Fat:** 19g, **Carbohydrate:** 80g, **Protein:** 12g

Upside-Down Apples

¼ cup finely chopped pecans or walnuts
¼ cup chopped dried apricots or any dried fruit
½ teaspoon ground cinnamon
½ teaspoon vanilla
¼ teaspoon ground nutmeg
⅛ teaspoon salt
2 tablespoons honey or maple syrup
2 Fuji apples (about 8 ounces each), halved and cored
1 cup vanilla sugar-free ice cream

1. Preheat oven to 350°F. Coat 9-inch pie pan with nonstick cooking spray.

2. Combine pecans, apricots, cinnamon, vanilla, nutmeg and salt in prepared pan; mix well. Spread evenly over bottom of pan. Drizzle with honey. Place apple halves in nut mixture, cut side down. Cover with foil.

3. Bake 35 minutes or just until tender. Spoon nut mixture over each apple half. Serve with ice cream.   *Makes 4 servings*

Tip: Fuji apples are a cross between Red Delicious and Ralls Janet apples. They are crisp and juicy apples that hold their shape when baking. If Fuji apples are not available, substitute Braeburn or Gala apples.

NUTRIENTS PER SERVING: Fiber: 4g, Calories: 187, Fat: 7g, Carbohydrate: 32g, Protein: 4g

---

Upside-Down Apple

Oatmeal Date Bars

2 packages (18 ounces each) refrigerated oatmeal raisin cookie
  dough
2½ cups old-fashioned oats, divided
2 packages (8 ounces each) chopped dates
1 cup water
½ cup sugar
1 teaspoon vanilla

1. Let both doughs stand at room temperature about 15 minutes. Preheat oven to 350°F. Lightly grease 13×9-inch baking pan.

2. For topping, combine three fourths of 1 package of dough and 1 cup oats in medium bowl; beat until well blended. Set aside.

3. For crust, combine remaining 1¼ packages of dough and remaining 1½ cups oats in large bowl; beat until well blended. Press dough evenly onto bottom of prepared pan. Bake 10 minutes.

4. Meanwhile, for filling, combine dates, water and sugar in medium saucepan; bring to a boil over high heat. Boil 3 minutes; remove from heat and stir in vanilla. Spread date mixture evenly over partially baked crust; sprinkle evenly with topping mixture.

5. Bake 25 to 28 minutes or until bubbly. Cool completely in pan on wire rack. *Makes about 2 dozen bars*

NUTRIENTS PER SERVING: **Fiber:** 3g, **Calories:** 281, **Fat:** 9g, **Carbohydrate:** 49g, **Protein:** 4g

Oatmeal Date Bars

Oatmeal Crème Brûlée

4 cups water
3 cups quick oats
½ teaspoon salt
6 egg yolks
½ cup granulated sugar
2 cups whipping cream
1 teaspoon vanilla
¼ cup packed light brown sugar
Fresh berries (optional)

SLOW COOKER DIRECTIONS

1. Coat slow cooker with nonstick cooking spray. Cover and set on HIGH. Meanwhile, bring water to a boil in small saucepan over high heat. Immediately pour into preheated slow cooker. Stir in oats and salt; cover.

2. Combine egg yolks and granulated sugar in small bowl; mix well. Heat cream and vanilla in medium saucepan over medium heat until mixture begins to simmer (small bubbles will begin to form at edge of pan). *Do not boil.* Remove from heat. Whisk ½ cup hot cream into egg yolk mixture until blended. Whisk warmed egg mixture back into cream until blended. Spoon mixture over oatmeal. *Do not stir.*

3. *Turn slow cooker to LOW.* Line lid with two paper towels. Cover; cook on LOW 3 to 3½ hours or until custard is set.

4. Sprinkle brown sugar over surface of custard. Line lid with two dry paper towels. Cover; cook on LOW 10 to 15 minutes or until brown sugar is melted. Serve with fresh berries, if desired.   *Makes 4 to 6 servings*

NUTRIENTS PER SERVING: Fiber: 4g, Calories: 588, Fat: 37g, Carbohydrate: 56g, Protein: 10g

Oatmeal Crème Brûlée

Almond-Pear Strudel

¾ cup slivered almonds
5 to 6 cups thinly sliced crisp pears (4 to 5 medium pears)
1 tablespoon grated lemon peel
1 tablespoon lemon juice
⅓ cup plus 1 teaspoon sugar, divided
2 teaspoons ground cinnamon
1 teaspoon ground nutmeg
6 sheets phyllo dough
¼ cup (½ stick) butter, melted
½ teaspoon almond extract

1. Preheat oven to 300°F. Spread almonds in shallow baking pan. Bake 6 to 8 minutes or until lightly browned, stirring frequently. Set aside.

2. Place pears in large microwavable bowl. Stir in lemon peel and lemon juice. Microwave on HIGH 6 minutes or until tender; cool. Combine ⅓ cup sugar, cinnamon and nutmeg in small bowl; set aside.

3. Cover work surface with plastic wrap. Place 1 phyllo sheet in middle of plastic wrap. (Cover remaining phyllo dough with damp kitchen towel to prevent dough from drying out.) Brush 1 teaspoon melted butter onto phyllo sheet. Place second phyllo sheet over first; brush with 1 teaspoon butter. Repeat layering with remaining sheets of phyllo.

4. *Raise oven temperature to 400°F.* Spray baking sheet with nonstick cooking spray. Drain pears and toss with sugar mixture and almond extract.

5. Spread pear mixture evenly over phyllo, leaving 3-inch strip on far long side. Sprinkle pears with ½ cup almonds. Brush strip with 2 teaspoons butter. Beginning at long side of phyllo closest to you, carefully roll up jelly-roll style, using plastic wrap to gently lift, forming strudel. Place strudel, seam side down, on prepared baking sheet. Brush top with 1 teaspoon butter.

6. Bake 20 minutes or until golden. Brush with remaining butter. Sprinkle with remaining ¼ cup almonds and 1 teaspoon sugar. Bake 5 minutes. Cool 10 minutes before serving. *Makes 8 servings*

NUTRIENTS PER SERVING: Fiber: 5g, Calories: 283, Fat: 13g, Carbohydrate: 42g, Protein: 4g

Whole Wheat Date Bars

4½ cups chopped dates
2½ cups water
2¾ cups whole wheat flour
 ¼ cup all-purpose flour
 2 cups old-fashioned oats
 ¼ cup packed brown sugar
1½ teaspoons salt
 ½ teaspoon ground cinnamon
 ½ cup maple syrup
 ½ cup (1 stick) cold butter, cut into very small pieces
 1 cup vegetable shortening, at room temperature

1. Preheat oven to 400°F. Grease or coat 13×9-inch baking dish with nonstick cooking spray.

2. Cook and stir dates and water in large saucepan over medium heat 10 minutes or until thickened to jam-like consistency. Remove from heat.

3. Combine whole wheat flour, all-purpose flour, oats, brown sugar, salt and cinnamon in large bowl. Stir in maple syrup. Cut butter into flour mixture with pastry blender or two knives until coarse crumbs form. Mix in shortening until dough holds together.

4. Place 5 cups dough into prepared baking dish. Press firmly on bottom and partially up sides of dish to form crust. Pour date mixture evenly into crust. Top with remaining dough.

5. Bake 25 minutes or until golden brown. Cool slightly before cutting into bars.
Makes 2 dozen bars

NUTRIENTS PER SERVING: Fiber: 5g, Calories: 304, Fat: 13g, Carbohydrate: 47g, Protein: 4g

Mango-Raspberry Crisp

1 mango, peeled, seeded and chopped into ½-inch pieces
1 cup fresh raspberries
½ cup old-fashioned oats
2 tablespoons packed brown sugar
½ to 1 teaspoon ground cinnamon
4 teaspoons butter
2 tablespoons chopped pecans

1. Preheat oven to 400°F. Spray four 6-ounce custard cups or ramekins with nonstick cooking spray.

2. Divide mango and raspberries evenly among custard cups.

3. Combine oats, brown sugar and cinnamon in medium bowl. Cut in butter with pastry blender or two knives until mixture resembles coarse crumbs. Stir in pecans. Sprinkle evenly over fruit.

4. Bake 20 to 25 minutes or until fruit is tender and topping is golden brown. Let stand 15 minutes before serving.   *Makes 4 servings*

Tip: Here's the easy "porcupine" method for getting nice pieces of mango without having to peel it. Stand the mango vertically on end on a cutting board. Cut off the two meaty mango cheeks on either side of the long flat pit by slicing down about an inch from the center on each side. If you hit the pit, move the knife over a little. Once you have the two round mango halves, lay them flat and cut through the flesh, but not the skin, in a cross-hatch pattern. Then turn each mango half inside out to make a "porcupine" of raised chunks. Carefully cut them away from the skin and into a bowl.

NUTRIENTS PER SERVING: Fiber: 4g, Calories: 171, Fat: 7g, Carbohydrate: 27g, Protein: 2g

Mango-Raspberry Crisp

Whole Grain Cranberry Chocolate Chip Cookies

1½ cups uncooked five-grain cereal
1 cup whole wheat flour
½ teaspoon salt
½ teaspoon baking soda
¼ teaspoon baking powder
½ cup (1 stick) unsalted butter, softened
⅓ cup packed light brown sugar
1 egg
½ teaspoon vanilla
½ cup golden raisins
½ cup semisweet chocolate chips
½ cup dried cranberries, chopped

1. Preheat oven to 350°F. Coat nonstick cookie sheet with nonstick cooking spray. Combine cereal, flour, salt, baking soda and baking powder in medium bowl.

2. Beat butter and brown sugar in large bowl with electric mixer until light and fluffy. Beat in egg and vanilla until well combined. Beat in flour mixture. Fold in raisins, chocolate chips and cranberries. Drop dough by tablespoonfuls 2 inches apart onto prepared cookie sheet.

3. Bake in center of oven 7 to 9 minutes or until golden. Transfer cookies to wire rack to cool completely.   *Makes about 18 cookies*

Variations: Substitute other multigrain cereal for the five-grain cereal. For additional flavor variations, you can also experiment with other dried fruit, such as dried apricots or cherries. Just be sure to chop the fruit well to evenly distribute it among the cookies.

NUTRIENTS PER SERVING: Fiber: 4g, Calories: 182, Fat: 8g, Carbohydrate: 28g, Protein: 3g

Whole Grain Cranberry Chocolate Chip Cookies

Pears with Apricot-Ginger Sauce

¼ cup water
4 whole firm pears (about 2 pounds total), peeled with stems
   attached
1 tablespoon lemon juice
2 tablespoons apricot fruit spread
1 teaspoon grated fresh ginger
½ teaspoon cornstarch
½ teaspoon vanilla

SLOW COOKER DIRECTIONS

1. Coat slow cooker with nonstick cooking spray. Add water. Arrange pears stem side up. Spoon lemon juice over pears. Cover; cook on HIGH 2½ hours.

2. Remove pears; set aside.

3. Combine fruit spread, ginger, cornstarch and vanilla in small bowl; stir until cornstarch dissolves. Add mixture to water in slow cooker, whisking until blended. Cover; cook on HIGH 15 minutes or until sauce thickens slightly. Spoon sauce over pears. Serve warm or at room temperature.

Makes 4 servings

Tip: Pears are one of the few fruits that can be picked while hard. They actually improve in texture and flavor after picking. Pears are ideal fruits for poaching since they soften, but don't become mushy or disintegrate after cooking. Spooning lemon juice over the peeled pears prevents them from discoloring.

NUTRIENTS PER SERVING: Fiber: 5g, Calories: 120, Fat: <1g, Carbohydrate: 31g, Protein: 1g

Pears with Apricot-Ginger Sauce

White Chocolate Pudding Parfaits

2 cups reduced-fat (2%) milk
1 package (4-serving size) white chocolate sugar-free instant pudding and pie filling mix
¾ cup cold whipping cream
1½ cups fresh raspberries or sliced strawberries
2 tablespoons chopped roasted shelled pistachio nuts or chopped toasted macadamia nuts

1. Combine milk and pudding mix in medium bowl; beat 2 minutes. Refrigerate 5 minutes or until thickened. Beat whipping cream in clean bowl with electric mixer at high speed until stiff peaks form. Fold whipped cream into pudding.

2. Layer ¼ cup pudding and 2 tablespoons raspberries in each of 4 parfait glasses; repeat layers. Spoon remaining pudding over berries. Serve immediately or cover and refrigerate up to 6 hours before serving. Sprinkle with nuts just before serving. *Makes 4 servings*

Tip: Raspberries are one of the fruits highest in fiber. They are also high in Vitamin C, B2, riboflavin, folate and niacin. While they are very perishable, fortunately raspberries freeze well. Wash and dry the berries and then freeze them in a single layer on a baking sheet. Once frozen, you can transfer the berries to a freezer bag. They will keep for up to a year.

NUTRIENTS PER SERVING: Fiber: 4g, Calories: 286, Fat: 21g, Carbohydrate: 19g, Protein: 7g

---

White Chocolate Pudding Parfaits

Cranberry Peach Almond Crisp

2 bags (16 ounces each) frozen unsweetened peach slices
1 cup dried cranberries
1 teaspoon vanilla
½ teaspoon almond extract
½ cup old-fashioned oats
⅓ cup packed dark brown sugar
¼ cup all-purpose flour
½ teaspoon ground cinnamon
¼ cup (½ stick) cold butter
¼ cup slivered almonds

1. Preheat oven to 350°F. Thaw peaches in microwave according to package directions; do not drain. Transfer fruit to 9-inch deep-dish pie pan or baking pan. Add cranberries, vanilla and almond extract. Stir gently to combine.

2. Combine oats, brown sugar, flour and cinnamon in medium bowl. Cut in butter with pastry blender or two knives until mixture resembles coarse crumbs. Stir in almonds; sprinkle mixture evenly over peaches.

3. Bake 40 minutes or until peaches are tender and top is golden brown.

Makes 6 servings

NUTRIENTS PER SERVING: Fiber: 5g, Calories: 321, Fat: 11g, Carbohydrate: 53g, Protein: 4g

Cranberry Peach Almond Crisp

METRIC CONVERSION CHART

VOLUME MEASUREMENTS (dry)

$1/8$ teaspoon = 0.5 mL
$1/4$ teaspoon = 1 mL
$1/2$ teaspoon = 2 mL
$3/4$ teaspoon = 4 mL
1 teaspoon = 5 mL
1 tablespoon = 15 mL
2 tablespoons = 30 mL
$1/4$ cup = 60 mL
$1/3$ cup = 75 mL
$1/2$ cup = 125 mL
$2/3$ cup = 150 mL
$3/4$ cup = 175 mL
1 cup = 250 mL
2 cups = 1 pint = 500 mL
3 cups = 750 mL
4 cups = 1 quart = 1 L

VOLUME MEASUREMENTS (fluid)

1 fluid ounce (2 tablespoons) = 30 mL
4 fluid ounces ($1/2$ cup) = 125 mL
8 fluid ounces (1 cup) = 250 mL
12 fluid ounces ($1 1/2$ cups) = 375 mL
16 fluid ounces (2 cups) = 500 mL

WEIGHTS (mass)

$1/2$ ounce = 15 g
1 ounce = 30 g
3 ounces = 90 g
4 ounces = 120 g
8 ounces = 225 g
10 ounces = 285 g
12 ounces = 360 g
16 ounces = 1 pound = 450 g

DIMENSIONS

$1/16$ inch = 2 mm
$1/8$ inch = 3 mm
$1/4$ inch = 6 mm
$1/2$ inch = 1.5 cm
$3/4$ inch = 2 cm
1 inch = 2.5 cm

OVEN TEMPERATURES

250°F = 120°C
275°F = 140°C
300°F = 150°C
325°F = 160°C
350°F = 180°C
375°F = 190°C
400°F = 200°C
425°F = 220°C
450°F = 230°C

BAKING PAN SIZES

Utensil	Size in Inches/Quarts	Metric Volume	Size in Centimeters
Baking or Cake Pan (square or rectangular)	8×8×2	2 L	20×20×5
	9×9×2	2.5 L	23×23×5
	12×8×2	3 L	30×20×5
	13×9×2	3.5 L	33×23×5
Loaf Pan	8×4×3	1.5 L	20×10×7
	9×5×3	2 L	23×13×7
Round Layer Cake Pan	8×1½	1.2 L	20×4
	9×1½	1.5 L	23×4
Pie Plate	8×1¼	750 mL	20×3
	9×1¼	1 L	23×3
Baking Dish or Casserole	1 quart	1 L	—
	1½ quart	1.5 L	—
	2 quart	2 L	—

GLENCOE

Solving Business Problems
Using a Calculator

Sixth Edition

Mildred K. Polisky